Private Sector Engagement for Sustainable Development

LESSONS FROM THE DAC

This work is published under the responsibility of the Secretary-General of the OECD. The opinions expressed and arguments employed herein do not necessarily reflect the official views of OECD member countries.

This document and any map included herein are without prejudice to the status of or sovereignty over any territory, to the delimitation of international frontiers and boundaries and to the name of any territory, city or area.

Please cite this publication as:
OECD (2016), *Private Sector Engagement for Sustainable Development: Lessons from the DAC*, OECD Publishing, Paris.
http://dx.doi.org/10.1787/9789264266889-en

ISBN 978-92-64-26687-2 (print)
ISBN 978-92-64-26688-9 (PDF)

The statistical data for Israel are supplied by and under the responsibility of the relevant Israeli authorities. The use of such data by the OECD is without prejudice to the status of the Golan Heights, East Jerusalem and Israeli settlements in the West Bank under the terms of international law.

Corrigenda to OECD publications may be found on line at: *www.oecd.org/about/publishing/corrigenda.htm*.

Foreword

In 2015, the global community set an ambitious agenda to realise sustainable development through adopting the Addis Ababa Action Agenda on financing for development, the 2030 Agenda and its Sustainable Development Goals, and the Paris Agreement on climate change. Taken together, these agreements outline a pathway to sustainability for our planet, prosperity and equity for all, and a new approach to working together in partnership.

All sectors – government, civil society, academia and the private sector – are working together to realise sustainable development. However, the scale and scope of the challenges facing the global community mean that going forward, there is a need for more and better multi-stakeholder partnerships to harness the best of what partners across sectors can offer to develop innovative solutions, mobilise private finance and promote better investments for sustainable development.

Many members of the Organisation for Economic Co-operation and Development's Development Assistance Committee (DAC) have a long history of working with the private sector to leverage private capital, expertise, core business and market-based solutions to meeting the challenge of making development sustainable. For others, private sector engagement is relatively new to their development co-operation portfolios. Regardless of their levels of experience, DAC members are looking for new and better ways to engage the private sector in development co-operation through the use of private sector instruments, policy dialogue and partnerships including many stakeholders.

Private sector engagement for sustainable development: Lessons from the Development Assistance Committee *draws on the experience of DAC members to identify emerging trends, good practice and lessons. The result of a range of peer learning activities, the report makes a timely contribution as DAC members and others expand, refine and consolidate approaches to private sector engagement. Grounded in practical experiences and the latest evidence, the report – and its associated resources – examines the political, policy and institutional foundations for engaging with the private sector, provides guidance on establishing and maintaining a portfolio of ways in which to engage the private sector, and shares practical approaches to minimising risk and realising results.*

The first of a series of thematic reviews launched by the DAC to increase peer-to-peer learning, the DAC peer learning review on working with and through the private sector has been a resounding success. It was grounded in a clear framework for analysis that reflected the needs and interests of DAC members for a review that was both policy and operationally relevant.

Going forward, the DAC will continue to engage with members and others on the important role of the private sector in development co-operation, and highlight and promote good practice. The DAC will also support further peer-to-peer learning among members, recognising the valuable contribution that such opportunities present to improving our approaches to development co-operation and, ultimately, realising better results.

Charlotte Petri-Gornitzka
DAC Chair

Acknowledgements

This report is the result of a peer learning exercise amongst all members of the OECD Development Assistance Committee. The OECD would like to express its appreciation to the governments of Germany, the Netherlands, Sweden and the United States for hosting country reviews, and for sharing their experiences; and the governments of Denmark and Luxembourg for hosting thematic workshops. Appreciation is also extended to the "peer learners" from Australia, Austria, Denmark, Luxembourg, the Netherlands, Korea and Sweden, as well as staff from the Development Co-operation Directorate (DCD) at the OECD, for their participation in the country reviews as well as their valuable comments on this report and related materials.

Private sector engagement for sustainable development: Lessons from the Development Assistance Committee (DAC) *was authored by Shannon Kindornay, Adjunct Research Professor at Carleton University and independent consultant, under the overall guidance of Rahul Malhotra (OECD, DCD). Managerial advice and support was provided by Karen Jorgensen (OECD, DCD). The team has been assisted by Kristin Sazama, Elizabeth Del Bourgo and Stephanie Coic (OECD, DCD), as well as Rachel Savard and Meghan Blom, research assistants that supported Ms Kindornay.*

The report was edited by Michael Olender and typeset by Peter Vogelpoel.

Table of contents

Figures

Table

Boxes

Acronyms and abbreviations

AECF	Africa Enterprise Challenge Fund
BBP	Vocational Education and Training Partnership Programme
BIO	Belgian Investment Company for Developing Countries
BMZ	Federal Ministry for Economic Cooperation and Development (Germany)
CSO	Civil society organisation
CSR	Corporate social responsibility
DAC	Development Assistance Committee
DEG	German Investment and Development Corporation
KVP	Chambers and Associations Partnership Programme
Sida	Swedish International Development Agency
SEK	Swedish Krona
SME	Small and medium-sized enterprise
ODA	Official development assistance
OECD	Organisation for Economic Co-operation and Development
OPIC	Overseas Private Investment Corporation
PPP	Public-private partnership
USAID	United States Agency for International Development

Executive summary

Member countries of the Organisation for Economic Co-operation and Development's (OECD) Development Assistance Committee (DAC) are increasingly developing partnerships with the private sector to leverage private capital, expertise, innovation and core business to benefit sustainable development. To learn from this experience and complement DAC peer reviews, the DAC introduced an in-depth, thematic peer learning review on working with and through the private sector. The review aims to identify good practice and lessons in private sector engagement.

The full peer learning report offers a wide range of lessons and a dedicated webpage has been launched to showcase the range of outputs from the peer learning review.[1] Here, we highlight 15 critical lessons.

1. *Communicate the who, what, when, where and how.*

A coherent narrative matched with clear communication of objectives, activities and results is a success factor in the implementation of private sector engagement strategies. Strategies should align with the overall focus and principles for development co-operation, including in terms of countries and sectors of focus, and facilitate policy coherence for development.

2. *Engage the private sector as a means, not an end.*

Development objectives and desired results should determine the selection of partners. The Sustainable Development Goals offer an important guiding framework in this regard. The decision to partner with the private sector should be rooted in a theory of change that establishes whether and how the private sector is best placed to help realise specific development results.

3. *Integrate aid effectiveness principles in private sector engagements.*

Ensuring private sector engagement opportunities are open to private sector partners from all countries facilitates country ownership, alignment, harmonisation and value for money.

4. *Ensure institutions are fit for purpose.*

Private sector engagement in development co-operation requires lead time, capacity and the right incentives for the effective adoption and evolution of strategies and tools. Capacity building is important for headquarter and field staff who pursue private sector engagements through approaches that make use of centralised and decentralised engagement mechanisms. Implementation of private sector engagement mechanisms should be carried out by government institutions such as aid agencies and development finance institutions according to their comparative advantages. Co-ordination between institutions on private sector engagement needs to be established.

5. *Invest in the business-enabling environment.*

Business-enabling environments in partner countries impact the possibilities for private sector engagement and the promotion of pro-development investments. Traditional forms of co-operation to improve business-enabling environments, such as technical assistance, remain critical.

6. *Develop a holistic, flexible portfolio of private sector engagement mechanisms that harness core business.*

The use of a range of engagement mechanisms, including financial mechanisms such as debt instruments, guarantees and grants as well as non-financial mechanisms such as policy dialogue and technical assistance, is an effective way to coherently address development challenges. A strategic approach harnesses core business, realises synergies across mechanisms, avoids unnecessary proliferation of engagement mechanisms by working with others where possible, and allows for experimentation and evolution. Making mechanisms adaptable to different contexts ensures that they are fit for purpose and maximises the impacts of partnerships.

7. *Include partner country governments.*

Partner country government perspectives should inform country-level private sector engagement activities. Such inclusion is critical for ensuring aid effectiveness since partner country engagement promotes country ownership and local buy-in, as well as country-level capacity to engage with the private sector.

8. *Facilitate private sector engagements with a wide range of stakeholders.*

The possibilities for private sector engagement differ according to the results sought in development co-operation and the capacities of different private sector partners. Approaches to engaging large companies as opposed to small and medium-sized enterprises, or domestic private sector partners as opposed to those in partner countries, will necessarily need to differ. Non-profit implementing partners require resources to effectively engage the private sector in development co-operation.

9. *Make it easy to engage.*

Opportunities for engagement should be clearly communicated to private sector partners. Strategies to facilitate private sector engagement include the establishment of partnership focal points and active promotion of engagement opportunities through, for example, business membership organisations.

10. *Level of effort should be proportionate to the benefits of engagement.*

The level of effort required for private sector partners to access engagement mechanisms should be proportionate to their benefits. For example, mechanisms that provide smaller funding amounts should make use of streamlined, simplified proposal processes compared to those that provide larger-scale funding on market terms. Government institutions should ensure that screening processes, support mechanisms, additionality assessments, and monitoring and evaluation requirements are proportionate to the size of their investments.

11. *See partnership as a relationship not a contract.*

The growth and expansion of new partnerships require maintenance of relationships. By establishing relationships, development partners can build trust with potential partners, engage more easily in exchanges on potential projects and work through co-creation processes.

12. *Take risks if you want others to do so.*

Government institutions must be willing to take risks if they want to encourage the private sector to do likewise. Clear criteria for partnership, evidence-based decision making and due diligence, including efforts to assess the motivations of potential partners, and the portfolio approach to private sector engagement are important risk management strategies. Effective communication of successes and failures helps ensure external stakeholder buy-in for greater risk profiles in government institutions.

13. *Leverage is about more than just money.*

Though leverage is often understood in financial terms, some DAC members note that it is important to understand leverage in terms of tangible and intangible impacts. The process of engagement changes mindsets in the private sector and approaches to conducting core business. Engagement has potential for long-term effects beyond any individual partnership, including the finance leveraged from the private sector.

14. *Establish systems to ensure and measure additionality.*

Systems for ensuring additionality when working with and through the private sector are important. A systematic approach to additionality assessment contributes to ensuring that private sector partnerships do not harm in terms of their environmental, social and economic impacts, effectively harnessing the comparative advantages of government institutions and realising better development results.

15. *Invest in results measurement and systems for monitoring and evaluation.*

The effective tracking of private sector engagement activities requires new and updated data management and information systems to track allocations, leverage and results. Targeted efforts are needed to identify and measure results within projects and for portfolios and move beyond monitoring the levels of mobilised finance. Efforts to define consistent and shared results indicators across private sector engagements are key in this regard.

There is a need to establish provisions for monitoring and evaluation at the outset of partnerships that are proportionate to their size and needs. The application of appropriate independent evaluation processes is important for assessing development impacts, communicating results, institutional learning and driving evidence-based decision making.

Note

1. For the full suite of private sector peer learning outputs, see: www.oecd.org/dac/peer-reviews/private-sector-engagement-for-sustainable-development-lessons-from-the-dac.htm.

Chapter 1

Introducing peer learning on working with and through the private sector in development co-operation

Development Assistance Committee (DAC) members are increasingly working with the private sector in development co-operation to realise sustainable development outcomes. This chapter introduces the DAC peer learning review on working with and through the private sector in development co-operation that was undertaken over 2015-16. It notes the importance of private sector engagement in development co-operation in light of successive international agreements aimed at facilitating greater financing for development, realising the Sustainable Development Goals and combating climate change. The chapter presents the methodology that informs the key findings highlighted in this report. The peer learning review drew on a range of research methodologies, including a literature review, survey of DAC members and others, four in-depth country reviews and three workshops.

Introduction

The important role of the private sector in realising sustainable development outcomes is well recognised by the international development community. Development stakeholders, including partner country governments, bilateral and multilateral aid agencies, international financial institutions and civil society organisations (CSOs), are working with private sector partners in development co-operation to harness private finance, job creation and service delivery potential, innovation and expertise to address sustainable development challenges (Di Bella et al., 2013). Private sector actors are also increasingly seeing sustainable development outcomes as critical to long-term business sustainability and profit maximisation (WBCSD, 2010; Accenture Strategy, 2016).

Recent agreements by the international development community, including the Addis Ababa Action Agenda on financing for development (UN, 2015a), the 2030 Agenda and its Sustainable Development Goals (UN, 2015b), and the Paris Agreement on climate change (UNFCCC, 2015), have recognised the essential role of the private sector in ensuring sustainable social, economic and environmental outcomes. Indeed, the scale and complexity of today's sustainable development challenges require a multi-stakeholder approach that draws on contributions from all parts of society – government, the private sector and civil society.

In this context, member countries of the Organisation for Economic Co-operation and Development's (OECD) DAC are increasingly developing partnerships with the private sector to leverage private capital, expertise, innovation and core business to benefit sustainable development. To learn from this experience and complement DAC peer reviews, the DAC introduced an in-depth, thematic peer learning review on working with and through the private sector. The review aims to identify good practice and lessons in private sector engagement.

This report is structured into six chapters. This chapter outlines the methodology and approach for the review. Chapters 2-6 provide an overview of the key themes and lessons across the main elements of the analytical framework that inform the overall review. Chapter 2 examines the building blocks for private sector engagement, namely politics, policies and institutions. Chapter 3 provides an overview of the focus and delivery of private sector engagements, while Chapter 4 focuses on the range of engagement tools used by DAC members and includes an overview of a new typology for understanding the modalities used in private sector engagements. Chapter 5 looks at partners in private sector engagements and draws out key lessons in terms of supporting successful multi-stakeholder partnerships. Chapter 6 provides an overview of how DAC members can move from risk to results in private sector engagements and addresses a number of areas including risk management, leverage, additionality, results management, and monitoring and evaluation. The report also includes an annex of key definitions and terminology used in the peer learning review, this report and other peer learning outputs.

In addition to the report, a number of resources have been made available online through a dedicated website on the peer learning review.[1] A short document that highlights good practice is available. Country reports on each of the four in-depth country reviews are also available. Each report provides an overview of the country's overall approach to private sector engagement, followed by a description of lessons that emerged from the review and a list of key resources such as policy documents, operational documents and evaluations. Four policy briefs have also been published as part of the peer learning review. They examine select critical issues: what is included in a holistic toolbox for private sector engagement; capacity development for private sector engagement; results, monitoring and evaluation; and private sector engagement in the context of environmental sustainability and climate change. In addition, the website provides two inventories. The first includes an overview of a new typology for understanding private sector engagement, including key terms and definitions used in the peer learning review. The second inventory provides a list of private sector engagement evaluations carried out or planned by DAC members. Finally, examples of particularly innovative mechanisms for engaging the private sector and specific partnerships are available. Submitted by reviewed countries, mechanism and partnership profiles provide basic information on scope and objectives, partners, activities, results, monitoring and evaluation, and insights.

Overview of peer learning activities

The peer learning review was launched in April 2015 with a survey of all 29 DAC members and selected non-members to take stock of and better understand current priorities and practices. Twenty-nine responses were received, including 27 responses from DAC members. Following the survey, the OECD organised an inception workshop in June 2015 that convened private sector focal points from member country governments to share lessons and refine the analytical scope and desired outcomes of the review.

Four DAC members – Germany, the Netherlands, Sweden and the United States – volunteered to be reviewed. Australia, Austria, Denmark, Luxembourg, the Netherlands, Korea and Sweden participated as reviewers. Country visits lasted from four to five days. Over the course of a visit, reviewers met with a range of government actors including headquarter and field staff, implementing partners, and representatives from the private sector, academia and civil society. Discussions touched on all aspects of the analytical framework for the review, which is discussed below.

Two "spotlight" workshops were held to explore key areas of interest to DAC members. Denmark hosted a workshop on innovative mechanisms for private sector engagement, while Luxembourg hosted a workshop on additionality. The workshops were attended by representatives from DAC member development agencies, bilateral development finance institutions (DFIs), international financial institutions, academia and the OECD. Field visits for DAC peer reviews of Denmark and the United States in 2016 provided additional evidence from partner country perspectives.

The final report focuses largely on the practical experiences of DAC members, which are complemented by key findings from the latest literature where appropriate.

Analytical framework

The review focuses specifically on the role of the private sector as a partner for development. It does not focus on private sector development, which is an important sector for DAC members. Private sector development includes interventions aimed at establishing an enabling environment for business, addressing market failures, and supporting businesses and individuals to participate effectively in the local, regional and global economy. While private sector engagement occurs in this context, the peer learning review looked more broadly at private sector engagement in all sectors in which DAC members provide support.

An analytical framework was prepared to establish the scope for the review (Figure 1.1). The framework was constructed based on initial feedback from DAC members on their learning priorities through survey responses and at the inception workshop in June 2015. It was further refined based on feedback from DAC members, as well as inputs from staff working on related work streams at the OECD.

The analytical framework established broad parameters and questions to enable comparison among DAC members. The framework includes an examination of the building blocks of private sector engagement – policies, institutions and co-ordination mechanisms. It looks at the focus of private sector engagement activities in terms of resource allocations by sector, region and partners. The framework also looks at private sector engagements at three levels:

- The overall portfolio: The suite of private sector engagement tools used by a DAC member is examined, including financial and non-financial tools. In this context, the resources required to manage the overall portfolio, and strategies for mitigating risk and scaling innovation, are examined. In the analytical framework, this is captured under "tools for private sector engagement".
- Mechanisms: Specific mechanisms that have been developed by DAC members, such as guarantee programmes or policy dialogue mechanisms, are showcased and lessons emerging from the use of specific mechanisms are gathered. Referred to as "innovative private sector mechanisms" in the analytical framework.
- Partnerships: The analytical framework draws out lessons on establishing and managing successful partnerships with the private sector. Referred to as "learning from partnerships" in the analytical framework.

The final component of the analytical framework – measurement challenges – examines how DAC members measure leverage and ensure additionality in their engagements with the private sector. It also includes a review of results management systems as well as systems for monitoring and evaluation.

Definitions and terminology

There is a lack of shared terminology in private sector engagement among DAC members. As shown in Chapter 2, some DAC members have strategies for private sector development and use the term to refer to supporting the business-enabling environment in a developing country as well as direct partnerships. Others have separate private sector development and private sector engagement strategies.

The lack of agreement on terminology extends to basic concepts, such as the private sector, and more complex concepts like additionality. Participants debated the concept of

Figure 1.1. **Analytical framework: Peer learning review**

Building blocks for private sector engagement | **Policies, institutions and co-ordination mechanisms**

- Refers to the foundational aspects of working with and through the private sector.
- What are the political drivers behind private sector engagement? What are the main objectives and implications for policy development?
- What are the approaches used in partner selection?
- What institutional frameworks are in place for establishing partnerships?
- What do staff capacities look like and what are the resource needs (time, human and financial resources) to successfully implement private sector engagement programming?
- How does co-ordination occur within DAC member countries across institutions responsible for private sector engagement, with partner countries and with other DAC members?

Focus and delivery of private sector engagement strategies | **Allocations, country focus, sectors, cross-cutting themes and partners**

- Refers to basic information regarding implementation of the private sector engagements.
- What are the overall annual allocations by engagement instrument and how have they evolved historically?
- How are engagements allocated across countries? What are key considerations for working in different country contexts, particularly in fragile and conflict-affected states?
- How are engagements allocated across sectors? What are key considerations for different sectors, particularly when working with small and medium enterprises and in the informal sector?
- How does integration of cross-cutting themes in private sector engagements occur, namely in terms of the environment, gender, human rights and governance, and responsible business practice?
- What are the roles of implementing partners, namely the private sector, civil society, research institutions and international organisations?

Tools for private sector engagement in development | **Suite of engagement tools, resource requirements, risk, innovation and scale**

- Refers to the overall mix of private sector engagement mechanisms employed.
- Which financial mechanisms are used? Financial mechanisms include grants, loans, guarantees, equities, development bonds, insurance, etc.
- Which non-financial mechanisms are used? Non-financial forms of engagement include policy dialogue, knowledge sharing, technical assistance and capacity development.
- How are linkages made between instruments?
- What are the resource requirements for management of the overall portfolio?
- How is risk managed?
- What approaches are used to support innovation and scale up successes?

Innovative private sector engagement mechanisms | **In-depth review of specific engagement mechanisms**

- What are the resource requirements to manage specific mechanisms?
- What kinds of implementation guidelines are used?
- How are results defined and measured?
- What are the particularly innovative components of the mechanisms?

Learning from partnerships | **Lessons in partnership formation and managment**

- Case study examples of successful partnerships in practice.
- What are the main lessons learned in the effective establishment and management of partnerships with the private sector?

Measurement challenges | **Leverage, additionality, results, monitoring and evaluation**

- How are leverage and additionality guaranteed and measured?
- What are the actual results achieved? How are results systems structured? What lessons have been learned in defining results jointly across sectors?
- How do monitoring systems function, including approaches used, evidence, opportunities for course correction and lessons learned?
- How are evaluation systems structured, including approaches, evidence and organisational learning systems?

Source: Kindornay, S. and R. Malhotra (2016), *Engaging the private sector in development co-operation: Learning from peers. Development Co-operation Report 2016: The Sustainable Development Goals as Business Opportunities*, OECD Publishing, Paris, http://dx.doi.org/10.1787/dcr-2016-en.

the private sector at the workshop on innovative mechanisms. Though they agreed that the private sector includes a range of different actors from entrepreneurs to multinational companies, there was a discussion about whether the term should be used strictly for for-profit entities. Moreover, it is unclear how some concepts such as innovative financing, blended finance and social impact investing relate to one another.

Given the lack of agreement on key concepts, shared terminology across DAC members in the area of private sector engagement would be helpful. At the very least, it could contribute to shared understandings when a particular term is used, facilitate comparison of activities across DAC members and enable more standardised reporting.

As mentioned, this report includes an annex of key definitions and terminology used in the peer learning review. The list of terms is meant to situate readers of the report. The definitions draw directly or have been adapted from the OECD Glossary of Statistical Terms where possible, as well as academic and policy literature (including from DAC members) on private sector engagement in development co-operation. As such, unless otherwise stated, the definitions in the annex are not official OECD definitions.

Note

1. For the full suite of private sector peer learning outputs, see: www.oecd.org/dac/peer-reviews/private-sector-engagement-for-sustainable-development-lessons-from-the-dac.htm.

References

Accenture Strategy (2016), "UN Global Compact-Accenture Strategy CEO study", www.accenture.com/us-en/insight-un-global-compact-ceo-study (accessed 29 June 2016).

Di Bella, J. et al. (2013), "Mapping private sector engagements in development cooperation, The North-South Institute, Ottawa, www.nsi-ins.ca/publications/mapping-private-sector-engagements-in-development-cooperation.

Kindornay, S. and R. Malhotra (2016), "Engaging the private sector in development co-operation: Learning from peers", *Development Co-operation Report 2016: The Sustainable Development Goals as Business Opportunities*, OECD Publishing, Paris, http://dx.doi.org/10.1787/dcr-2016-en.

UN (2015a), "Addis Ababa action agenda of the Third International Conference on Financing for Development", United Nations, New York, www.un.org/esa/ffd/wp-content/uploads/2015/08/AAAA_Outcome.pdf.

UN (2015b), "Transforming our world: the 2030 agenda for sustainable development", A/RES/70/1, United Nations, New York, https://sustainabledevelopment.un.org/post2015/transformingourworld.

UNFCCC (2015), "Adoption of the Paris Agreement", United Nations Framework Convention on Climate Change, Paris, https://unfccc.int/resource/docs/2015/cop21/eng/l09.pdf.

WBCSD (2010), "Business and development: Challenges and opportunities in a rapidly changing world", World Business Council for Sustainable Development, Geneva, www.wbcsd.org/pages/edocument/edocumentdetails.aspx?id=42&nosearchcontextkey=true.

Private Sector Engagement for Sustainable Development:
Lessons from the DAC

Chapter 2

Building blocks for private sector engagement in development co-operation

This chapter examines the politics, policies and institutional dimensions of private sector engagement in development co-operation. Political drivers for private sector engagement include the need to harness other sources of finance to address sustainable development challenges, ambitions to benefit from private sector-inspired solutions to development challenges and the desire to support domestic commercial interests while realising development results in partner countries. The promotion of domestic commercial interests as part of private sector engagements in development co-operation has two implications. On one hand, it undermines aid effectiveness. On the other hand, the integration of policy objectives can create opportunities for better policy coherence and more policy coherence for development, with development considerations becoming a greater focus in trade and foreign policy. The review of policies for private sector engagement revealed the importance of a coherent narrative matched with clear communication of objectives, activities and results as an important success factor in implementation. Finally, with respect to institutional dimensions, the peer learning review showed that private sector engagement in development co-operation requires lead time, capacity development and the right incentives for the effective adoption and evolution of strategies and tools. Also, ensuring coherence and knowledge sharing between government implementing partners requires mechanisms for regular co-ordination.

Politics

There is a variety of drivers behind the increasing focus on the private sector as a partner in development. Di Bella et al. (2013) provide a useful overview of the key drivers for private sector engagement. First, as a proportion of development finance, aid has decreased significantly in recent years when compared to trade, foreign direct investment and remittances. Though aid has continued to increase, with a few exceptions,[1] the scale and scope of global sustainable development challenges has prompted DAC members, as well as others, to consider how limited aid resources can best harness other sources of development finance. The financing needs for the 2030 Agenda, which are set to be in the trillions, have further propelled sentiments regarding the need to harness other sources of development finance, in particular from the private sector.

Second, fiscal austerity in DAC member countries, now compounded by overwhelming flows of Syrian refugees into European DAC member countries, has put pressure on aid budgets. In this context, DAC members are looking to leverage aid budgets through innovative financing mechanisms, market-based solutions to development challenges and direct partnerships with the private sector.

Third, in addition to leveraging private sector finance, DAC members are looking to benefit from the expertise, innovative solutions, and possibilities for technology spillover, job creation and service delivery presented by private sector partners. By harnessing core business activities to be more inclusive and sustainable, there is significant potential to harness shared value between the interests of development and commercial actors (see e.g. Lucci, 2012). Moreover, DAC members see private sector engagement as a way to improve cost effectiveness and value for money.

Fourth, there is an opportunity for development partners to harness movement within the private sector toward responsible business. Though motivations for engagement in development vary for different types of private sector partners, such as multinational companies, large domestic companies, and small and medium-sized enterprises (SMEs) (Gradl, Sivakurmaran and Sobhani, 2010), companies are increasingly seeing their long-term sustainability as tied not only to the economic outcomes of their operations, but also social and environmental outcomes. As such, companies are seeking to engage in development in terms of their core operations and through philanthropic commitments to social causes (Kindornay, Higgins and Olender, 2013).

Finally, DAC members are also motivated to work with the private sector given the increasing recognition that developing and emerging countries are key markets and investment sites for DAC member countries' companies and investors (CAFOD, 2013; Heinrich, 2013; Kindornay and Reilly-King, 2013; Byiers and Rosengren, 2012). In this context, partnership with the private sector offers an opportunity for DAC members to promote development objectives while benefiting their own commercial sectors. For some DAC members, the recognition has led to concerted efforts to establish greater coherence between development, trade and investment portfolios.

The peer learning review revealed that DAC members are motivated to varying extents by the various drivers outlined above. The promotion of domestic commercial interests is likely the most contentious of these drivers. A number of DAC members have developed private sector instruments that are tied to their own private sectors. The aim of this approach is to support two objectives: development and the promotion of domestic commercial interests. Even in cases where private sector engagement mechanisms are not formally tied to domestic private sector partners, many DAC members tend to work most with their own private sector partners because innovative and risky partnerships require mutual confidence and trust between participating government and private stakeholders. As such, it can be easier to initiate engagements with private stakeholders from within DAC member countries since partners often already know one another and proximity allows greater opportunities for collaboration.

Political pressure to ensure that private sector engagements benefit DAC members' domestic private sectors has a number of implications for policy and practice. On one hand, it raises the question of how DAC members' interests can be balanced with existing DAC member commitments to aid effectiveness, including untied aid. The peer learning review revealed that the use of development co-operation to support domestic commercial interests in provider countries undermines aid effectiveness, in particular ensuring country ownership, alignment, harmonisation and value for money. Domestic actors are not always the best placed to realise country-owned development outcomes and provide the best value for money. Moreover, a focus on domestic commercial interests undermines co-ordination with other DAC members that continue to uphold the commitment to untied aid. If DAC members focus on their own commercial interests, it is more difficult for them to harmonise efforts, co-ordinate, pool resources and pursue joint initiatives. During the review, some DAC members noted that engagement with the private sector should align with existing DAC member commitments to aid effectiveness, particularly untied aid.

The peer learning review revealed that the use of development co-operation to support domestic commercial interests in provider countries undermines aid effectiveness, in particular ensuring country ownership, alignment, harmonisation and value for money.

On the other hand, the promotion of poverty reduction, sustainable development and domestic commercial interests are not necessarily mutually exclusive. The country review of the Netherlands showed that the integration of multiple policy objectives can lead to greater policy coherence for development. In the Netherlands, increased private sector engagement has been driven, in part, by the goal of better integrating Dutch companies into the global economy. The combination of development and trade objectives is managed by one minister who is mandated to facilitate greater coherence. This approach has led to changes in terms of a greater focus on trade and Dutch companies in the Netherlands' development co-operation. However, it has also led to changes in trade policy. Corporate social responsibility (CSR) efforts are now more effectively integrated into trade-related activities and sectoral policy discussions. Good CSR has become a pre-condition for engagement by the private sector in development activities.

Policies

The survey of DAC members showed that they are at different stages in terms of the extent to which they engage the private sector in development co-operation. Some members have been engaging the private sector for decades, while for others, private sector engagement is a relatively new endeavour. As such, DAC members take different approaches in policy frameworks for private sector engagement. Some members have no dedicated policy on private sector engagement, others have one or very few policies, while others have a wide range of policies that cover different forms of private sector engagement. Annex A provides an overview of DAC member strategies according to responses to the survey.[2] Some DAC members have policies that specifically target private sector engagement, while others incorporate private sector engagement as part of a private sector development strategy. While the review focuses on private sector engagement, strategies related to private sector development have been included below to illustrate the range of approaches taken by DAC members.

As shown in Annex A, 15 surveyed DAC members have specific policy frameworks or strategies to engage the private sector. Another seven DAC members refer to private sector engagement in broader policy documents or on their websites, though have not made available a formal strategy. Generally speaking, these frameworks outline DAC members' ambition to harness the private sector's finance, innovation and know-how through strategies that capitalise on the alignment of development and commercial objectives. The survey revealed three main objectives in DAC member policy frameworks:

- leveraging private sector funds and capacities toward development-oriented investments
- promoting collaboration between domestic and partner country private sector actors; and
- promoting private sector development in partner countries.

These objectives are not mutually exclusive and many DAC members seek to promote all three.

DAC members are making use of financial mechanisms such as guarantees, debt instruments and grants, implemented by themselves or other partners, to promote development-friendly investments in partner countries in a range of sectors, as noted below. Here, private sector engagement relates to the "how" of development co-operation. In this sense, the objective of leveraging the private sector is about engagement with the private sector to realise development outcomes through a range of sector-agnostic tools. In terms of the second objective, business-to-business schemes are used to promote collaboration between domestic and partner country private sector actors. These schemes typically provide financial and technical support for business-to-business partnerships.

Finally, as shown in Annex A, many DAC members include the promotion of private sector development alongside private sector engagement in their strategies. These approaches include activities directed at establishing sound business environments, addressing market failures, and supporting individuals and businesses to effectively engage in the economy. Strategies for private sector development often include financial and non-financial forms of private sector engagement, such as financial support and capacity development for private sector partners in partner countries, as well as knowledge and technology transfer programmes.

The review of private sector engagement strategies shows that DAC members continue to make limited reference to aid effectiveness principles in their policy frameworks for private sector engagement, as noted by Kindornay and Reilly-King (2013) in their study of DAC member policies. The limited reflection on aid effectiveness and effective development co-operation principles in private sector engagements is a significant gap in dac member policy frameworks.

Effective communication on private sector engagement

DAC members take a range of policy approaches to private sector engagement. Some have no overarching policy while others have a range of policies. A lesson emerging from the peer learning review is that a coherent narrative matched with clear communication of objectives, activities and results is an important success factor in the implementation of private sector engagement strategies. The focus and objectives, activities, and results of private sector engagements should be clearly articulated and communicated to all stakeholders inside and outside government. In cases where objectives, activities and results were not clearly articulated, the review revealed inconsistencies in a number of areas. In some instances, private sector engagement activities were not sufficiently linked to the overall focus and principles for development co-operation. Moreover, inconsistencies were apparent between policy makers and implementing partners in terms of their understandings of private sector engagement and how it should be carried out.

A coherent narrative matched with clear communication of objectives, activities and results is an important success factor in the implementation of private sector engagement strategies.

The review also showed the importance of transparency on private sector engagements for external stakeholders. Indeed, a key critique of DAC members in this context has been the lack of transparency and communication on the objectives, mechanisms and results of private sector engagements (see e.g. Kindornay and Reilly-King, 2013; Di Bella et al., 2013; Romero, 2014; ActionAid et al., 2015; Pereira, 2015). Communication of strategies and results is the basis for engagement with critics and champions of private sector engagement. The United States noted that continued communication over time is necessary to allay concerns, share lessons and results, and bolster support for the approach.

Comparative advantages in approaches to private sector engagement

The review also showed the importance of grounding policies and approaches to private sector engagement in comparative advantages. As demonstrated below, private sector engagement requires a range of skills and capacities. By focusing on areas where comparative advantages exist, DAC members can link existing expertise to the facilitation of private sector engagements, thereby leveraging their own knowledge and positioning themselves as expert partners for the private sector.

In the Netherlands, private sector engagements tend to fall under three main areas – private sector development (including infrastructure), food security and water. Sectoral specialisations have facilitated the development of skills within government institutions to engage the private sector and have ensured that the government can serve as a relevant partner by contributing finance, sectoral expertise and knowledge of local contexts.

In its approach to private sector engagement, Germany aims to harness its economic strengths – SMEs, the vocational education system and well-developed business membership organisations (chambers of commerce and business associations). The government works with business membership organisations to support similar organisations in developing countries, develop vocational education programmes and promote investment opportunities in developing countries.

Institutions

The peer learning review examined a range of institutional factors that influence the successful implementation of private sector engagement efforts. It looked at leadership, organisational culture, capacities and resourcing, decision making within institutions and between headquarter and field staff, and co-ordination. Unlike other aspects of private sector engagement in development co-operation, institutional factors have received less attention in the academic and policy literature.[3] The review makes a contribution in this regard and provides practical insights on institutional dimensions of private sector engagement in development co-operation.

Leadership

Buy-in from the top levels within aid agencies is critical for private sector engagement. Leadership by the director-general at the Swedish International Development Agency (Sida) and chief executive officers in partner companies has helped to push forward such engagement. In the United States, presidential directives and initiatives that place a clear emphasis on private sector engagement have created momentum within and between institutions responsible for development co-operation to work individually and together with the private sector.

Though high-level leadership is important, country reviews also revealed the importance of leadership and ownership over private sector engagement for staff in country and those responsible for thematic strategies. Embassies and operational units have country and sectoral expertise that should inform private sector engagements and can help establish and manage partnerships in relation to existing strategies.

Organisational culture

Though some DAC members have long-established programmes for private sector engagement, for many others, the integration of private sector engagements into regular operations and development portfolios is new. For some institutions, this approach will require changes in mindset and culture. The country review of Sweden revealed the importance of dedicating time and resources to ensuring that stakeholders understand the value of private sector engagements and have shared terminology, information and expertise to recognise and pursue new opportunities. Staff responsible for supporting the integration of private sector engagements throughout Sida operations noted that good examples of successful partnerships create more openness among staff to partnering with the private sector.

Capacity and resourcing

A key lesson across all of the country reviews is that private sector engagement requires lead time, capacity development and incentives for the effective adoption and evolution of strategies and tools. This lesson applies to countries that are newer to private sector engagement, such as Sweden, and countries with a longer history of experience such as the United States, Germany and the Netherlands.

Private sector engagement requires lead time, capacity development and incentives for the effective adoption and evolution of strategies and tools.

Effective systems to ensure that institutions are fit for purpose – such as through appropriate staffing, co-ordination mechanisms, and data and information systems – take time to be established. When new mechanisms and approaches are being established, growing pains translate into higher transaction costs at the outset. It takes time to develop shared terminology, build capacities and build trust between actors within and outside of government to realise policy objectives. Moreover, approaches to private sector engagement evolve over time as institutions learn from past experiences, staff rotate, new private sector partners emerge and the nature of sustainable development challenges changes. As such, an iterative process for private sector engagement can emerge requiring ongoing reflection on and review of institutional operations and capacities. The length of time needed to establish private sector engagement mechanisms and individual partnerships should not be underestimated.

The survey of DAC members revealed that the majority of respondents (21) have staff specifically working on private sector issues either through dedicated units or across institutions (Figure 2.1). For those that stated their staffing profile, the majority noted that their staff have previous experience in working within a private sector entity. Others indicated that their staff members have a mix of skills, including experience in co-operation with private sector entities, development finance, agriculture and social protection. Two respondents indicated that they carried out or will carry out a capability assessment of existing and needed expertise in their institutions to engage the private sector.

Though all of the reviewed countries have dedicated staff working on private sector engagement, the challenge of ensuring that appropriate capacities are in place was highlighted across the reviews. Countries noted difficulties in ensuring that enough staff

Figure 2.1. **Number of DAC members with different staffing profiles for private sector engagement**

are dedicated to private sector engagement in comparison to the ambitions of agendas, building broad-based institutional capacities including at headquarter and field levels, and ensuring ongoing capacity development opportunities, given staff turnover and rotation. Moreover, new mechanisms for private sector engagement are typically developed at headquarter level, which means that embassies often need additional support to develop understanding of them and capacities to make use of them.

There are a number of strategies to ensure that institutions are appropriately equipped. First, institutions can recruit directly from the private sector. Second, some institutions have developed systems for continued training and skills development to build internal capacity. An effective approach in this regard, which is used by Sweden (Box 2.1) and the United States, is the use of dedicated focal points or units and resources that provide support and training to other units to ensure that all staff have the ability to identify opportunities, understand when interests are aligned with those of the private sector, and know what tools are available for partnership. Finally, some institutions have also made use of secondments to the private sector and from the private sector to build internal capacity.

Box 2.1. **Equipping staff to effectively engage the private sector: Sweden's approach**

As private sector engagement became an increasing priority for Sweden, Sida took a number of steps to build capacities across the agency and at the country level. These steps included the development of specific training programmes and secondments of junior experts to embassies. Given the decentralised model for private sector engagement, Sweden's capacity development activities have included a focus on the capacities of staff working in partner countries.

Sida and embassy staff received training in planning and implementation of private sector engagement activities as well as creating and developing dialogue with the local private sector and other relevant actors. Sida's loans and guarantee team rolled out a capacity development programme with colleagues, making use of international training packages and e-learning. In addition to the provision of ongoing training activities, Sida's unit for private sector collaboration and partnerships provides support to embassies and sectoral specialists on private sector engagement.

In 2012, Sida invested in a programme to second junior experts to embassies in developing countries for periods of two to three years. Their role was to educate embassy staff on private sector engagement and work with them to identify opportunities.

The approach to capacity development may be impacted by the structure of private sector mechanisms and how they are developed. With centrally managed private sector mechanisms, it is important to have well-resourced contact or entry points at headquarter level to enable embassy staff to ask for advice, identify opportunities and ensure effective co-ordination.

It should also be noted that private sector engagement does not only require the development of technical skills within institutions. Soft skills – interpersonal skills, flexibility and adaptability, communication, and resourcefulness – are critical to successful private sector engagements. Good relationships and relationship management are key factors in private sector engagement. The country review of the United States showed that soft skills are important for engaging across sectors, but also in terms of relationships between headquarter and field staff and US government institutions.

Soft skills – interpersonal skills, flexibility and adaptability, communication, and resourcefulness – are critical to successful private sector engagements.

In addition to ensuring that the right capacities are in place, it is important to develop operational approaches and incentives to promote the integration of private sector engagement across institutions. The inclusion of units responsible for private sector engagement in the establishment of sectoral, bilateral and regional development co-operation plans offers one means to further integrate private sector engagement across development portfolios.

Some institutions have adopted overall targets as a means to incentivise greater private sector engagement across sectors and at the country level. In the United States' experience, mandating private sector engagement through the use of targets can be an important way to facilitate and encourage the use of specific mechanisms, notably private sector instruments. However, this approach can also create incentives to meet input targets, rather than the goal of maximising development impacts. As such, target setting in relation to leverage ratios or the number of private sector engagement activities that will be carried out by institutions should be used in conjunction with a clear focus on development results.

In the case of Sweden, the absence of a specific budget for working with and through the private sector provides incentives for Sida staff to work with the private sector only when it is the most effective partner in delivering on objectives. While this approach is beneficial on one hand, on the other, a specific budget may be needed to test new ideas and innovative mechanisms as well as integrate these into the activities of institutions.

Systems fit for purpose: Harnessing comparative advantages and co-ordination

As DAC members move forward with developing and expanding their private sector engagement portfolios, it is important to make use of the comparative advantages of government and other implementing partners when deciding how new mechanisms will be implemented. There is a need to clearly define roles and harness comparative advantages.

The management of private sector engagement mechanisms should be determined by institutions' existing networks, expertise and experience. For example, some government institutions operate private sector engagement programmes that support domestic objectives which could be internationalised and adapted for development co-operation. Bilateral DFIs and international financial institutions have significant experience in engaging the private sector, particularly in terms of providing loans, guarantees, equity, risk insurance and technical assistance. On the other hand, aid ministries and agencies have expertise in working with other kinds of implementing partners and partner country governments as well as supporting enabling environments for private sector investment in partner countries. To avoid duplication of efforts and ensure efficiency in private sector engagements, the comparative advantages of implementing partners should inform the development of strategies and activities. Once selected, a clear division of labour is critical between policy makers and implementing partners to ensure that activities are efficiently carried out.

Adopt mechanisms for regular co-ordination between institutions on private sector engagement.

Some of the country reviews also revealed a lack of co-ordination with respect to private sector engagement across government entities responsible for development co-operation. Given that private sector engagements are carried out using a diverse range of government implementing partners, such as DFIs and specialised agencies, and that co-ordination is not automatic, there is a need to adopt mechanisms for regular co-ordination between institutions on private sector engagement. The establishment of formal and informal mechanisms for government institutions to discuss experiences and strategise on private sector engagements offers opportunities for continuous and joint learning, knowledge exchange, and coherence and synergies across activities carried out by a diverse range of government entities. The use of shared data management and knowledge sharing platforms in the area of private sector engagement has potential to promote synergies within and between institutions. The US Feed the Future[4] initiative uses this approach – government institutions report against a shared results framework through a shared data portal. This approach facilitates alignment of activities and results reporting on the initiative. In the United States, whole-of-government initiatives have been a useful way to co-ordinate private sector engagements (Box 2.2).

Box 2.2. Ensuring co-ordination on private sector engagement through whole-of-government initiatives

In a complex system characterised by many government actors and other partners with differing interests and levels of capacity, a unified understanding of where initiatives are headed through clear guidance is important. In the United States, Presidential Directives and Initiatives have been important for facilitating whole-of-government approaches to private sector engagement. Presidential Directives and Initiatives provide overall direction to government institutions on the priorities of the government and have facilitated co-ordination across government institutions and between headquarters and field level. Under the Power Africa initiative, all relevant US government institutions are working toward improving access to electricity in Africa. The initiative is overseen by a co-ordinator who ensures coherence across activities.

Finally, the need for co-ordination extends beyond DAC member institutions responsible for development co-operation. International co-ordination between DAC members, including their DFIs, is important for harmonising efforts in relation to private sector engagement and furthering discussion on best practice. There are some initiatives that work to harmonise DAC members' efforts. For example, bilateral and multilateral DFIs have created a set of harmonised results indicators[5] that enable them to more efficiently and consistently analyse the impacts of projects, enhance opportunities for sharing best practices and lessons learned, and simplify reporting requirements for private sector partners that may engage with multiple DFIs. Throughout the peer learning review, it was noted by reviewed countries, reviewers and participants at the spotlight workshops that there is a need for further opportunities for discussion and co-ordination on issues related to private sector engagement in development among DFIs, as well as with aid ministries and agencies.

Notes

1. Total official development assistance (ODA) declined for the first time in 15 years in 2011 and then again in 2012. In 2013, ODA rebounded and has continued to grow, totalling USD 131.6 billion in 2015. See Love (2012) and OECD (2016) for details.
2. Slight updates have been made to accommodate DAC members that released new strategies since the survey was carried out.
3. The research that has been conducted on institutional and organisational factors has typically looked at these factors in relation to the functioning of partnerships, value creation therein or in relation to specific private sector instruments (see e.g. Copestake and O'Riordan, 2015; Kindornay, Tissot and Sheiban, 2014; Pattberg and Widerberg, 2014). This work has not touched on the specific and unique characteristics of aid ministries and agencies, including their decentralised structures, though insights from the research resonate with the broad literature on engagement between the public and private sectors.
4. For more information, see: www.oecd.org/dac/peer-reviews/Feed-the-Future.pdf.
5. See https://indicators.ifipartnership.org.

References

ActionAid et al. (2015), "Delivering sustainable development: A principled approach to public-private finance", Oxfam International, Oxford, www.oxfam.org/en/research/delivering-sustainable-development-principled-approach-public-private-finance.

Byiers, B. and A. Rosengren (2012), "Common or conflicting interests? Reflections on the private sector (for) development agenda", *Discussion Paper*, No. 131, European Centre for Development Policy Management, Maastricht, http://ecdpm.org/wp-content/uploads/2013/11/DP-131-Conflicting-Interests-Private-Sector-Development-Agenda-2012.pdf.

CAFOD (2013), "Public-private partnerships (PPPs) in international development – Are we asking the right questions?", Catholic Agency for Overseas Development, London, http://cafod.org.uk/content/download/9569/77021/version/2/file/PPP-interactive.pdf.

Copestake, J. and A. O'Riordan (2015), "Challenge funds in international development: Definitions, variations and research directions", *Public Administration and Development*, No. 35, pp. 1-18.

Di Bella, J. et al. (2013), "Mapping private sector engagements in development cooperation, The North-South Institute, Ottawa, www.nsi-ins.ca/publications/mapping-private-sector-engagements-in-development-cooperation.

European Commission (2014), "Communication from the Commission to the European Parliament, the Council, the European Economic and Social Committee and the Committee of the Regions: A stronger role of the private sector in achieving inclusive and sustainable growth in developing countries", 13.5.2014/COM(2014)263 final, European Commission, Brussels, http://eur-lex.europa.eu/legal-content/EN/TXT/PDF/?uri=CELEX%3A52014DC0263&qid=1400681732387&from=EN.

Global Affairs Canada (2016), "Private sector as partners in development", Government of Canada, Ottawa, www.international.gc.ca/development-developpement/partners-partenaires/ps-sp.aspx?lang=eng (accessed 1 July 2016).

Gradl, C., S. Sivakumaran and S. Sobhani (2010), "The MDGs: Everyone's business", United Nations Development Programme, New York, https://business.un.org/en/documents/8652.

Heinrich, M. (2013), "Donor partnerships with business for private sector development: What can we learn from experience?", The Donor Committee for Enterprise Development, Cambridge, www.enterprise-development.org/wp-content/uploads/DCEDWorkingPaper_PartnershipsforPSDLearningFromExperience_26Mar2013.pdf.

Kindornay, S., K. Higgins and M. Olender (2013), "Models for trade-related private sector partnerships for development", The North-South Institute, Ottawa, www.nsi-ins.ca/publications/models-for-trade-related-private-sector-partnerships-for-development.

Kindornay, S. and F. Reilly-King (2013), "Investing in the business of development: Bilateral donor approaches to engaging the private sector", The North-South Institute and Canadian Council for International Co-operation, Ottawa, www.nsi-ins.ca/publications/investing-in-the-business-of-development.

Kindornay, S., S. Tissot and N. Sheiban (2014), "The value of cross-sector development partnerships", The North-South Institute, Ottawa, www.nsi-ins.ca/wp-content/uploads/2014/01/The-Value-of-Cross-Sector-Development-Partnerships.pdf.

Love, P. (2012), "Development aid drops for the first time in 15 years," *OECD Insights*, OECD Publishing, Paris, http://oecdinsights.org/2012/04/04/development-aid-drops-for-the-first-time-in-15-years.

Lucci, P. (2012), "Post-2015 MDGs: What role for business?", Overseas Development Institute, London, www.odi.org/publications/6645-post-2015-millennium-development-goals-role-business.

Ministry of Foreign Affairs of the Netherlands (2015), "Ministry of Foreign Affairs vision on sustainable trade", Ministry of Foreign Affairs of the Netherlands, The Hague.

OECD (2016), "Development aid rises again in 2015, spending on refugees doubles", OECD Publishing, Paris, www.oecd.org/dac/development-aid-rises-again-in-2015-spending-on-refugees-doubles.htm (accessed 1 July 2016).

Pattberg, P. and O. Widerberg (2014), "Transnational multi-stakeholder partnerships for sustainable development: Building blocks for success", IVM Institute for Environmental Studies, Amsterdam, http://fragmentation.eu/wp-content/uploads/2014/08/R14-31-ICSC-report-FINAL.pdf.

Pereira, J. (2015), "Leveraging aid: A literature review on the additionality of using ODA to leverage private investments", UK Aid Network, London, www.ukan.org.uk/wordpress/wp-content/uploads/2015/03/UKAN-Leveraging-Aid-Literature-Review-03.15.pdf (accessed 8 June 2016).

Romero, M. (2014), "A private affair: Shining a light on the shadowy institutions giving public support to private companies and taking over the development agenda", European Network on Debt and Development, Brussels, www.eurodad.org/files/pdf/1546237-a-private-affair-shining-a-light-on-the-shadowy-institutions-giving-public-support-to-private-companies-and-taking-over-the-development-agenda.pdf (accessed 8 June 2016).

Private Sector Engagement for Sustainable Development:
Lessons from the DAC

Chapter 3

Focus and delivery of private sector engagement strategies in development co-operation

This chapter examines the focus of private sector engagement strategies and their delivery. It begins with a discussion of the difficulties related to capturing a full picture of private sector engagements in development co-operation. DAC members target countries eligible for official development assistance (ODA) or focus on specific target countries in their private sector engagements. They also tend to target economic infrastructure and services as the top sector for engagement. Though private sector engagement is possible in all countries and sectors, the review revealed the importance of aligning the geographic and thematic focus of private sector engagements with overall strategies for development co-operation. This approach ensures coherence across development co-operation programming and ensures that donors have the necessary expertise and resources to effectively engage with partners. To ensure effectiveness and relevance, private sector engagement tools should be catered to country type and context.

Overall flows for private sector engagement

Complete figures on private sector engagement in development co-operation are unavailable. Private sector engagement occurs in a variety of ways through financial and non-financial mechanisms. Policy dialogue, for example, is not necessarily counted in official figures because it does not always involves a financial flow. Private sector engagement activities implemented through CSOs and multilateral implementing partners are counted as ODA with no specific marker to indicate that the flows are related to engagement with a private sector partner. Figures on non-concessional finance are also incomplete since not all financial institutions report to the OECD and information that is provided is often incomplete (OECD, 2015a).

In an effort to better capture private sector engagement in development co-operation and promote its use, the DAC has agreed to better reflect in ODA the donor effort involved in the use of private sector instruments (OECD, 2016e). This effort is also likely to improve reporting on private sector engagement because DAC members will be asked to provide activity-level reporting on relevant operations. Moreover, the DAC also agreed to report data on amounts mobilised from the private sector as part of its regular data collection. The OECD's work on a new measure of total official support for sustainable development will also reflect the amounts that DAC members leverage from the private sector.[1]

Existing figures and analysis from the OECD provide some indication of DAC members' allocations in relation to private sector engagement. In terms of non-concessional flows, Klein, Sangaré and Semeraro (2014) show that concessional finance from international financial institutions tends to go to least developed and low-income countries. Middle-income countries tend to benefit from non-concessional or other official flows. Economic infrastructure made up the largest sectoral share of these flows in 2012 (60%), followed by productive sectors (35%) and social infrastructure (5%) (Klein, Sangaré and Semeraro, 2014: 66). With respect to bilateral DFIs, data from the OECD for 2013 show that lower middle-income countries are the largest recipients of DFI financing, accounting for nearly 42%, followed by upper middle-income countries (34%), least developed countries (20.5%) and other low-income countries (3.75%) (OECD, 2016d). In terms of sector allocations in 2013, most allocations went to banking and financial services, energy generation and supply, industry and agriculture.

Kindornay and Reilly-King (2013) show that it can be more difficult to assess and compare private sector engagements through ODA. In addition to the issues noted above, the use of different concepts and terminology among DAC members further exacerbates the challenge of comparing and aggregating figures on private sector engagement. For example, the Netherlands reports its private sector engagement activities as part of its overall private sector development portfolio. This portfolio includes activities that support business-enabling environments in developing countries, including flows to governments and multilateral partners for technical co-operation, as well as direct partnerships with the private sector. The United States, on the other hand, reports figures on private sector partnerships and the amounts leveraged through its activities. Some DAC members do not report publicly on their private sector engagement portfolios at all. As mentioned in Chapter 6, there is a significant need for DAC members to update data collection processes and information management systems to ensure more effective reporting on private sector engagements in the future.

Geographic and sectoral focus

The survey of DAC members revealed that countries tend to take two main approaches to the geographic focus of their private sector engagement activities – mechanisms are either open to all ODA-eligible countries or targeted at focus countries. Many DAC members are prioritising countries in Africa in their engagement strategies. Some respondents also noted that least developed countries, low-income countries and fragile states are priorities.

Most survey respondents (20) noted that their interventions are largely concentrated in economic infrastructure and services, particularly energy generation and supply (many respondents indicated investment in green energy technologies) and other infrastructure (Figure 3.1). The productive sector, particularly interventions in agriculture, and the social sector – health and education specifically – were also highlighted. Nine respondents indicated that their interventions do not target specific sectors.

Figure 3.1. **Number of DAC members with different sectoral profiles for private sector engagement**

Social sector
7
Economic infrastructure and services
20
Productive sector
13
No specific sector
9

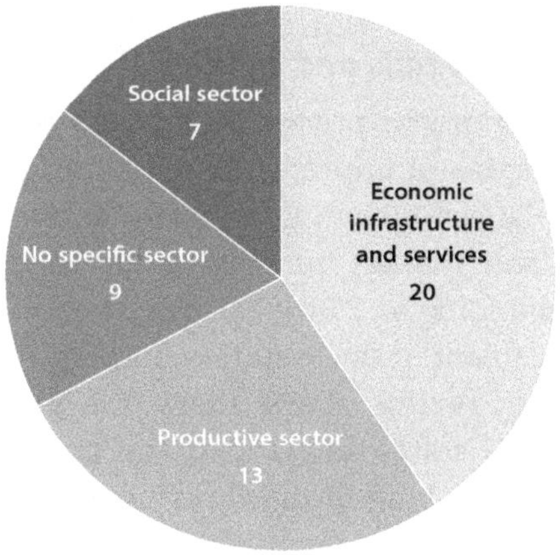

The focus of efforts

The geographic and sectoral focus of private sector engagements should align with overall strategies for development co-operation. DAC members face the challenge of ensuring that private sector engagement mechanisms are sufficiently driven by private sector demand to engage private sector partners while still aligning with more specific development priorities. Nevertheless, given that private sector engagement is a means to realise development objectives, rather than a goal in itself, engagement mechanisms should support overall development co-operation objectives. DAC members typically work in a wide enough range of countries and sectors to offer many opportunities for private sector partners to engage. Moreover, in instances where private sector interests do not align fully with the countries or sectors in which a DAC member works, DAC members can play a role in facilitating linkages and engagements between private sector actors and other DAC members for which greater alignment may exist. When mechanisms are open to all countries and sectors, possibilities to harness in-country and sectoral expertise, ensure alignment with partner country development objectives, and establish synergies across programmes and initiatives are diminished. Moreover, as noted in Chapter 5, part of what government institutions offer in their engagements with the private sector is country and sector expertise and networks. Untargeted approaches to private sector engagement may not sufficiently harness the contributions that government institutions make beyond finance.

Private sector engagement mechanisms can be more effective when catered to country type and context.

Alignment with existing country and sectoral priorities is also important given that private sector engagement mechanisms can be more effective when catered to country type and context, which often requires in-country presence or, at a minimum, expertise. Staff require deep country knowledge to identify viable opportunities and partners, as well as the ability to adapt engagement mechanisms to local contexts. For example, lower-income countries are often characterised by poor enabling environments, making it more challenging to promote investment. In these contexts, the mechanisms used may be fairly simple, such as grants or simple loan structures. Middle-income countries may offer possibilities for more sophisticated financing given more advanced regulatory environments.

Engaging the private sector in fragile and conflict-affected states

There is a range of challenges for private sector engagement in fragile and conflict-affected states, including weak and unpredictable institutions and legal environments, internal and external imbalances including large fiscal and trade deficits, corruption, instability, and limited reliable market information (Avis, 2016; International Dialogue on Peacebuilding and Statebuilding and BNP Paribas Investment Partners, forthcoming). Though private sector engagement in these states continues to be isolated in comparison to overall activities, a recent review of the literature on private sector engagement in fragile and conflict-affected states shows that the private sector can play a role in supporting stabilisation, spurring long-term economic growth and trade, and improving transparency (Avis, 2016).[2] As noted by the International Dialogue on Peacebuilding and Statebuilding and BNP Paribas Investment Partners (forthcoming), there is a need to change the narrative with respect to opportunities and risks for investors in fragile and conflict-affected states, improve market information, and make better use of development finance to incentivise private investment.

DAC members' practical experiences suggest that private sector engagement can be an effective tool for working in fragile and conflict-affected contexts, despite the challenges noted above. Promoting investments and partnerships in fragile and conflict-affected states requires specific mechanisms, incentives and criteria to attract private sector partners. Typically, government needs to be willing to take on greater risk. By taking on greater risk, donors and their development partners can improve development outcomes, contribute to market development, and have important demonstration effects in terms of crowding in investments by showing that it is possible to invest in fragile and conflict-affected contexts and make a return. Good examples of private sector collaboration in fragile and conflict-affected states show that it is possible to move beyond humanitarian, transition and traditional forms of grant-based aid, though these forms continue to play a critical role (Box 3.1).

Box 3.1. **Private sector engagement in fragile and conflict-affected states: Experience from the Africa Enterprise Challenge Fund**

The Africa Enterprise Challenge Fund (AECF) aims to facilitate pro-poor growth and poverty alleviation in Africa by making agribusiness, rural financial services and market systems work better for the poor. The fund expands entrepreneurs' access to finance to stimulate innovation and find profitable ways of improving access to markets and the way markets function for the poor, particularly the rural poor and smallholder farmers.

The AECF includes a Post-Conflict Window that aims to provide opportunities for applicants from post-conflict countries. Business ideas implemented in the Democratic Republic of the Congo, Liberia, Sierra Leone and Somalia/Somaliland are eligible for support. Competitions for AECF funding are open to for-profit private companies from anywhere in the world provided that their business ideas are implemented in Africa (or specific African countries for certain windows). Private companies are invited to compete for AECF funding by submitting new and innovative business ideas to a particular AECF window and competition. Ideas must comply with the rules on eligibility and selection criteria of the competition. Projects must be innovative, commercially viable, and have benefits for the rural poor in terms of increased incomes, job creation, reduced costs or improved productivity.

The AECF can provide up to USD 1.5 million per project in grants and interest-free loans that are repayable over the life of a project. Companies must provide matching funds (own resources or funds from partners or third parties, at least half of which must be cash and what remains can be in-kind) equal to or greater than 50% of the total cost of the project (the higher the percentage of own resources or funds from partners or third parties, the higher the probability of being selected). The Post-Conflict Window makes USD 12.5 million available for projects and has funded 20 projects as of July 2016 that focus on contract farming, processing, input supply, and trading, and has the highest proportion of indigenously owned business awardees compared to other windows.

Supporting entrepreneurs in fragile and post-conflict states has not been without its challenges. Businesses are often limited in size and capacity, which creates a challenge for AECF to identify high-quality partners with whom to work. In practice, AECF's grant management team has had to be flexible to effectively support grantees and allow them time to improve their business practices over the course of a grant. Moreover, the lack of commercial sources of finance means that more grant money may need to be disbursed up front and the definition of matching funds may need to be expanded to include existing assets rather than new investment; in this case, grants cover a larger portion of new project costs and, as such, increase donor risk. The lack of commercial financing also means that donors should consider opportunities for follow up funding to ensure that businesses can continue to operate once grant support ends. Though AEFC has seen success in its support to businesses in fragile and post-conflict states, a key lesson is that there is a "need for flexible risk management and the patience to pursue delayed benefits" (KPMG, 2013).

Sources: Mechanism profile, www.oecd.org/dac/peer-reviews/Africa-Enterprise-Challenge-Fund.pdf; KPMG (2013), "Risky business: Promoting private sector development in post-conflict states; Lessons from the Africa Enterprise Challenge Fund", Development in Practice: International Development Advisory Services Impact Paper, no. 12, KPMG, Nairobi, www.enterprise-development.org/wp-content/uploads/RiskyBusiness-PromotingPrivateSectorDevelopmentinPost-ConflictStates.pdf.

Engaging the private sector to respond to humanitarian crises

The United States has seen significant interest by the private sector to engage in the context of humanitarian crises. This experience has prompted the United States Agency for International Development (USAID) to reflect on key lessons to improve future engagements. The country review of the United States noted the importance of establishing clear expectations for partnership with private sector stakeholders in advance of humanitarian crises. In this context, it is important to be clear on where there are opportunities for partnership as opposed to procurement. Some private sector partners are interested mainly in procurement opportunities that involve the delivery of goods and services, whereas others are looking to contribute to projects and programmes as a partner. The development of memoranda of understanding with businesses on how co-operation will occur *a priori* is important for ensuring efficient and effective responses in times of crises. In addition, avenues for long-term recovery and resilience should be considered from the outset of humanitarian crises, including in terms of private sector engagements.

Engaging the private sector across sectors

Private sector engagement is possible in all sectors. The use of private sector engagement as a modality for co-operation, similar to others such as bilateral assistance or technical co-operation, opens up possibilities in all sectors. Using desired development results as a starting point, some DAC members have found that the private sector serves as an appropriate partner in traditional sectors for engagement such as private sector development, energy and infrastructure, but also in non-traditional sectors such as the environment, health and governance.

Private sector engagement is possible in all sectors.

All of the reviewed countries provided examples of private sector engagement in non-traditional sectors. Sweden made a deliberate choice to use horizontal, sector-agnostic mechanisms when relevant to achieve the goals of a particular strategy. One example of Swedish engagement with the private sector in a non-traditional sector is the Colombia Business in Development Facility Hub.[3] The hub promotes partnerships with the private sector to create, develop and expand income-generation projects in rural areas affected by armed conflict. It plays a role in contributing to stabilisation efforts in Colombia by promoting economic opportunities.

Germany is engaging the private sector to address migration challenges through programmes co-ordinated by the Federal Ministry for Economic Cooperation and Development (BMZ), Federal Employment Agency and Federal Ministry of Education and Research. In 2015-16, BMZ carried out a vocational education and training programme for young refugees in Germany in partnership with skilled crafts chambers as well as chambers of commerce and industry. The Federal Employment Agency has developed a programme that aims to inform young refugees about the German training and employment system and includes apprenticeship opportunities with Germany companies. In partnership with the Federal Ministry of Education and Research, the Federal Employment Agency is also training refugees in inter-company vocational training centres and companies. Refugees learn the language used in the crafts sector and receive support from social workers. The aim of the programme is to prepare up to 10 000 refugees for dual apprenticeship training within the skilled trades sector until 2018.

Outside of Germany, BMZ is also supporting a programme to enhance vocational training opportunities for Syrian refugees in Turkey. In order to improve capacities for reconstruction, Syrian refugees (as well as socially disadvantaged Turkish residents) will benefit from preparatory measures for employment, including language training and craft skills training. Partners on the initiative include German business membership organisations, such as skilled crafts chambers or chambers of commerce and industry, as well as business associations. The programme is designed for a first phase of three years with a grant of up to EUR 15 million and implemented by sequa with a main office in Ankara in close co-operation with Turkish authorities. There is potential to harness greater support for such initiatives across DAC members.

The Netherlands has provided support to the Health Insurance Fund (PharmAccess Foundation, n.d.). Managed by the PharmAccess Foundation, the Fund subsidises insurance premiums in order to facilitate access to basic health insurance for low-income groups in African countries. The programme has led to increased demand for pre-paid health schemes and, as such, improved investment opportunities in local health capacity. Health-care providers are providing better quality care as payment to them depends on their performance.

The United States is also working with the private sector in health. Helping Babies Breathe[4] is a public-private partnership (PPP) co-ordinated through ministries of health in partner countries that develops and implements evidence-based health-care practices to decrease neonatal mortality due to birth asphyxia in low-resourced countries. The partnership includes knowledge partners, CSOs and companies. Its training curriculum was developed by the American Academy of Pediatrics and early evidence was generated by the Eunice Kennedy Shriver National Institute of Child Health and Human Development and other health research institutions and associations. Johnson & Johnson trains birth attendants and Laerdal Global Health develops resuscitation devices, provides them at cost and improves supply chain logistics. Save the Children implements the partnership and Latter-day Saint Charities purchases training materials and equipment. Helping Babies Breathe has been introduced in over 77 countries and more than 300 000 birth attendants have been trained and equipped. Over a two-year period in Tanzania, it reported reductions in early newborn mortality (within the first 24 hours of life) by 47% and stillbirth by 24%.

Notes

1. See also Benn et al. (2016) for a review of the amounts mobilised from the private sector by official development finance interventions from guarantees, syndicated loans and shares in collective investment vehicles.
2. In particular, Avis (2016) notes that local private sector actors have a keen interest in stabilisation efforts because they tend to be more affected by conflict than large companies. As a potential partner in development co-operation, small local businesses tend to be more labour-intensive than large companies, better linked to other smaller businesses, and more likely to invest and expand locally in comparison to companies that operate internationally.
3. For more information, see: www.oecd.org/dac/peer-reviews/Colombia-Business-in-Development-Facility-Hub.pdf.
4. For more information, see: www.oecd.org/dac/peer-reviews/Helping-Babies-Breathe.pdf.

References

AECF (n.d.), Africa Enterprise Challenge Fund website, www.aecfafrica.org (accessed 1 July 2016).

Avis, W. (2016), "Private sector engagement in fragile and conflict-affected settings", GSDRC, Birmingham, www.gsdrc.org/wp-content/uploads/2016/03/HDQ1331.pdf.

Benn, J. et al. (2016), "Amounts mobilised from the private sector by official development finance interventions: Guarantees, syndicated loans and shares in collective investment vehicles", *OECD Development Co-operation Working Papers*, No. 26, OECD Publishing, Paris, http://dx.doi.org/10.1787/5jm3xh459n37-en.

International Dialogue on Peacebuilding and Statebuilding and BNP Paribas Investment Partners (forthcoming), "Investing in stability: Promoting more and better investment in post-conflict fragile and conflict-affected situations", OECD, Paris.

Kindornay, S. and F. Reilly-King (2013), "Investing in the business of development: Bilateral donor approaches to engaging the private sector", The North-South Institute and Canadian Council for International Co-operation, Ottawa, www.nsi-ins.ca/publications/investing-in-the-business-of-development.

Klein, A., C. Sangaré and G. Semeraro (2014), "The growing development potential of other official flows", *Development Co-operation Report 2014: Mobilising Resources for Sustainable Development*, OECD Publishing, Paris, http://dx.doi.org/10.1787/dcr-2014-en.

KPMG (2013), "Risky business: Promoting private sector development in post-conflict states; Lessons from the Africa Enterprise Challenge Fund", *Development in Practice: International Development Advisory Services Impact Paper*, no. 12, KPMG, Nairobi, www.enterprise-development.org/wp-content/uploads/RiskyBusiness-PromotingPrivateSectorDevelopmentinPost-ConflictStates.pdf.

OECD (2016a), "DAC High Level Meeting communiqué", OECD Publishing, Paris, www.oecd.org/dac/DAC-HLM-Communique-2016.pdf.

OECD (2016b), "Development finance institutions and private sector development", OECD Publishing, Paris, www.oecd.org/dac/stats/development-finance-institutions-private-sector-development.htm (accessed 1 July 2016).

OECD (2015), "Current reporting on private-sector instruments in DAC statistics", DCD/DAC(2015)27, OECD Publishing, Paris, www.oecd.org/officialdocuments/publicdisplaydocumentpdf/?cote=DCD/DAC(2015)27&docLanguage=En (accessed 4 June 2016).

PharmAccess Foundation (n.d.), "The Health Insurance Fund", https://www.pharmaccess.org/ (accessed 1 July 2016).

Private Sector Engagement for Sustainable Development:
Lessons from the DAC

Chapter 4

Tools for private sector engagement in development co-operation

This chapter begins with a presentation of a new typology for private sector engagements. Key lessons from the peer learning review are then presented on how DAC members establish private sector engagement mechanisms and the structure of private sector engagement portfolios, including the need for consultation and an examination of available human resources to implement such mechanisms. The critical need for DAC members to continue to support business-enabling environments alongside these mechanisms is highlighted. An overarching lesson for private sector engagement portfolios is that an effective approach is characterised by a mix of financial and non-financial private sector engagement mechanisms that are flexible, work together and are selected according to desired development results. This approach involves establishing and leveraging linkages between financial and non-financial engagement mechanisms, ensuring flexibility in implementation with balanced roles for headquarter and field staff to originate private sector engagements, and the selection of private sector mechanisms grounded in development priorities. Finally, experimentation and reflection on the effectiveness of such mechanisms is important since portfolios are being established and evolve over time.

A typology for private sector engagement in development co-operation

Through the peer learning review, DAC members identified the need for a shared typology to conceptualise private sector engagements in development co-operation. The discussion and new typology presented below are meant to contribute to the development of shared understandings of modalities and mechanisms. The typology aims to provide a shared terminology for discussions among DAC members with respect to their private sector engagements. It also provides a comprehensive framework against which DAC members can review such engagements, particularly in terms of identifying gaps in current approaches.

Exercises aimed at classifying private sector engagements in development are not new. Byiers and Rosengren (2012) suggest two categories for understanding private sector engagements: activities aimed at increasing private sector investment in development and those aimed at harnessing private sector finance for development. They situate tools that incentivise private sector investment by sharing risks such as challenge and innovation funds, grants, and other forms of subsidies into the first category. In the second category, they place leveraging mechanisms, namely PPPs, private equity and infrastructure funds. Kindornay and Reilly-King (2013) take as similar approach and categorise engagements according to their contributions to private sector development objectives, namely supporting business-enabling environments in developing countries, addressing market

Box 4.1. The role of the private sector in development co-operation

Beneficiary: Cases where the private sector benefits from development co-operation activities, including in terms of efforts to create an enabling business environment, financial support, capacity development, technical assistance, information provision and knowledge sharing.

Implementer: The private sector implements new business models to realise development impacts in terms of social, economic and/or environmental sustainability.

Reformer: The private sector reforms existing business approaches to be more development friendly in terms of social, economic and/or environmental sustainability.

Resource provider: Refers to instances when the private sector invests finance, expertise or other strategic resources. Includes donations and investments (financial and non-financial) in projects or initiatives that have a development objective.

Participant: Participation by the private sector in development-related initiatives including policy dialogue, knowledge sharing and multi-stakeholder initiatives.

Target: The private sector is targeted by government, civil society, other private sector stakeholders and/or multilateral organisations to change its business practices.

Source: Adapted from Vaes, S. and H. Huyse (2015), "Mobilising private resources for development: Agendas, actors and instruments", BeFinD Working Paper, No. 2, HIVA-KU Leuven, Leuven, www.befind.be/publications/WPs/WP2.

failures and investing in businesses and people. Germany's BMZ has also set out basic forms of co-operation organised according to the levels of risk undertaken by donors (BMZ, 2011b). Di Bella et al. (2013) and Smith (2013) look at modalities for engagement. The former classify private sector engagements according to broad categories that are sector and goal agnostic, while the latter links specific modalities to the types of objectives that they typically aim to achieve. Vaes and Huyse (2015) take a different approach by categorising private sector engagements in terms of the role of the private sector actor (Box 4.1).

Though they categorise partnerships and engagement tools differently, these studies show that there is a wide range of activities to engage the private sector. Drawing from and building on the typologies discussed above, the typology presented below aims to consolidate modalities and mechanisms within the context of private sector engagement. The typology is not exhaustive of all possible forms of private sector engagement. It focuses on private sector engagement from the view of development co-operation providers – the categorisation is based on the modalities and mechanisms provided by DAC members as the

Box 4.2. **Private sector instruments**

Grants: These include transfers in cash or in kind for which no legal debt is incurred by recipients. In the context of private sector engagement, DAC members provide grants directly to companies, including through challenge or innovation funds, as well as other implementing partners, such as CSOs and multilateral organisations, to carry out activities in partnership with private sector partners. Under the Creditor Reporting System, grants include standard grants, interest subsidies and capital subscriptions on deposit and encashment basis. See develoPPP.de[a] for an example.

Debt instruments: These include transfers in cash or in kind for which recipients incur legal debt. Debt instruments include standard loans, bonds, asset-backed securities and reimbursable grants. See the Dutch Good Growth Fund.[b]

Mezzanine finance instruments: Mezzanine finance can be structured as debt or preferred stock. It includes subordinated loans, preferred equity and other hybrid instruments.

Equity and shares in collective investment vehicles: Refers to investment in a country on the DAC List of ODA Recipients that is not made to acquire a lasting interest. Includes common equity, shares in collective investment vehicles and reinvested earnings.[c]

Guarantees and other unfunded liabilities: A guarantee refers to a risk-sharing agreement under which the guarantor agrees to pay part or the entire amount due on a loan, equity or other instrument to the lender/investor in the event of non-payment by the borrower or loss of value in case of investment. Other unfunded contingent liabilities refer to other instruments that do not constitute a flow as such but may be also collected in future. See Development Credit Authority.[d]

These private sector instruments can be used in the context of innovative financing, blended finance and impact investing.

Notes: Categories of instruments as described in the 2016 Converged Statistical Reporting Directives for the Creditor Reporting System (OECD, 2016a). See OECD (2016b) for definitions of specific instruments included in each broad category of private sector instruments. For a review of some of the more complicated financial instruments used by donors, see Benn et al. (2016) and Bilal et al. (2014, 14).

a. For more information, see: www.oecd.org/dac/peer-reviews/develoPPP-de.pdf.

b. For more information, see: www.oecd.org/dac/peer-reviews/Dutch-Good-Growth-Fund.pdf.

c. For more information, see: www.oecd.org/dac/peer-reviews/Micro-and-Small-Enterprise-Fund.pdf.

d. For more information, see: www.oecd.org/dac/peer-reviews/Development-Credit-Authority.pdf.

Table 4.1. **Typology of private sector engagement in development co-operation**

Modality	Objectives	Mechanisms	Examples[a]	Roles of the private sector	Level of financial risk
Knowledge and information sharing	• Advance solutions by sharing new methods, tools and innovative approaches to addressing development challenges	• Multi-stakeholder networks • Learning platforms • Conferences, seminars, workshops and other events • Funding for research (specifically on private sector engagement in development co-operation)	• Aligned Capital in Impact Investing • Alliance for Integrity • PPPLab • Practitioner Hub for Inclusive Business[b]	• Beneficiary • Participant • Resource provider	• Low
Policy dialogue	• Develop policy agendas and frameworks at international, national and local levels that reflect all parties' interests • Change behaviour such as through improvements in corporate practices and industry standard-setting	• Multi-stakeholder networks and platforms • Cross-sector roundtables • Specialised hubs or institutions • Institutionalised dialogues	• Dutch Post-2015 Charter Initiative • Inclusive Business Action Network • Swedish Leadership for Sustainable Development	• Beneficiary • Participant • Target	• Low
Technical assistance	• Enable private sector actors to effectively engage in development co-operation such as through support for project design • Improve private sector actors' operational capacities and effectiveness	• Business advisory services • Feasibility studies	• DEG financing opportunities • Service Point for the Private Sector and EZ-Scouts	• Beneficiary	• Moderate • Private sector beneficiaries typically contribute to costs
Capacity development	• Improve capacities of private sector actors to contribute to development results • Change or modify business operations	• Training activities and other forms of capacity development programming • Professional exchanges and secondments	• Chambers and Associations Partnership Programme (KVP) • Entrepreneurship promotion • Vocational Education and Training Partnership Programme (BBP)	• Beneficiary • Reformer • Target	• Low
Finance	• Leverage or raise private sector finance and investment promotion • Test innovation and scale success • Monetise development results (e.g. output-based mechanisms) • Support expansion of more and better business including through the promotion of business-to-business partnerships, inclusive business, responsible business conduct and CSR • Harness private sector expertise and market-based solutions to development challenges	• Private sector instruments including grants, debt instruments, mezzanine finance instruments, equity and shares in collective investment vehicles, guarantees and other unfunded liabilities • Includes the range of instruments captured under innovative finance	• African Enterprise Challenge Fund • African Guarantee Fund • DEG financing opportunities • Development Credit Authority • Dutch Good Growth Fund • Global Development Alliances • Impact investing	• Beneficiary • Implementer • Reformer • Resource provider • Participant	• Moderate to high

Notes: a. For private sector peer learning profiles, see: www.oecd.org/dac/peer-reviews/privatesectorengagementforsustainabledevelopmentlessonsfromthedac.htm.

b. For more information, see: www.inclusivebusinesshub.org/.

starting point. Nevertheless, it also refers to the role(s) of the private sector in each modality. The typology provides definitions for broad modalities for private sector engagement and the mechanisms used therein, notes the types of objectives that are often associated with modalities, outlines levels of private sector financial risk associated with each modality, and provides examples found online[1] (with one exception) for illustration. Depending on how mechanisms are structured, they can draw on multiple engagement modalities (e.g. by including policy dialogue and financing in one mechanism). Within each modality, engagements occur at various levels of depth, ranging from private sector collaboration to more formal private sector partnerships. Given that there is a range of mechanisms for the finance modality, Box 4.2 provides an overview of definitions of private sector instruments.

The lessons that arose from the peer learning review on the tools for private sector engagement pertain to how DAC members establish private sector engagement mechanisms, the types of mechanisms established, and how they are structured and relate to one another.

Establishing private sector engagement mechanisms: What to consider

Consultation

It is valuable to consult with stakeholders during the establishment of private sector engagement mechanisms. Engagement with the private sector is important for ensuring that new policies and engagement tools factor in the needs and interests of potential partners. Depending on the stakeholders targeted for engagement, there may be a need to consult with small to larger businesses and those domiciled in DAC member countries as well as partner countries. Consultation should also extend beyond the private sector to include inputs from partner country governments, civil society, knowledge institutions and other implementing partners that also participate in private sector engagements in development and have practical experience and lessons from research that can inform approaches.

Development and commercial objectives

It is also important to consider how to best balance development objectives and private sector interests in the structuring of mechanisms. A number of DAC members have established private sector demand-driven mechanisms for private sector engagement. In this context, private sector instruments are open and able to operate in multiple markets where opportunities exist. While this approach facilitates opportunities for businesses to identify and take advantage of opportunities in a wide range of countries, there is also a need to ensure that private sector engagement mechanisms are responsive to the development needs and objectives of partner countries. A balanced approach to the creation of private sector engagement portfolios can help in this regard through the inclusion of open mechanisms as well as those that are structured to respond to and meet demands also arising at the country level, including demands from local companies.

Existing private sector engagement mechanisms and gaps

When establishing new private sector engagement mechanisms, DAC members should pay attention to the existing suite of mechanisms offered by government institutions outside development co-operation. Governments offer a range of services and support to the private sector. During the country review of Germany, private sector partners noted that the develoPPP.de programme[2] fills an important gap by providing finance on a longer term (three years) than other government institutions and for direct investments in partner countries. As private sector engagement mechanisms and sustainable development challenges evolve, it is important to continue to review existing mechanisms in light of potential gaps between them. For example, specialised tools may be needed to target the smallest companies or promote impact investing (see e.g. impact investing by OPIC[3]). During the workshop on innovative mechanisms and in country reviews, DAC members noted that there are often financing gaps for small companies. Finance is available for subsidy programmes in start-up phases and larger finance amounts when scaling operations, but not during the stages in between when a company moves toward consolidation of activities, yet is still too small to access larger financing windows.

Another important issue is the supply of bankable projects. In many instances, potential partners require additional support to make potential projects bankable and mechanisms are not necessarily structured to provide support for project development.

Pay attention to the existing suite of mechanisms offered by government institutions outside development co-operation.

This issue raises the question of whether there are sufficient opportunities for potential partners to receive capacity development and technical assistance during the project development phase. There are at least two approaches that DAC members can take to address this issue in their engagement portfolios. The first is by ensuring support services are embedded into existing mechanisms or financial instruments are linked to other modalities such as technical assistance and capacity development. For example, DFIs commonly provide financing or technical assistance for feasibility studies, as well as other business support services. A second option is to dedicate funds specifically to bring projects from inception to bankability. The Overseas Private Investment Corporation (OPIC), the United States' DFI, recently launched the U.S.-Africa Clean Energy Finance Initiative in collaboration with other US government institutions to provide early stage support to project developers and investors in order to develop clean energy projects into bankable opportunities (OPIC, n.d.).

DAC members should also consider what is offered by other DAC members and multilateral organisations. There has been a proliferation of mechanisms to engage the private sector. Many DAC members have established private sector engagement mechanisms that offer similar opportunities to potential partners. These instruments are matched by those at the global level – many of which are funded by DAC members.

Going forward, there is a need for careful consideration in the creation of new instruments and for the consolidation of existing instruments. DAC members should not avoid creating their own mechanisms for private sector engagement altogether. Country contexts in DAC member countries as well as partner countries are diverse and therefore may necessitate new or revised mechanisms adapted to a specific context. Moreover, objectives also inform whether a new mechanism is needed. For example, when the objective of a mechanism is to support innovation, there may be a need for a new mechanism that tests particular types of innovations that are not captured by existing ones.

Working with like-minded DAC members and making use of existing instruments reduces duplication of efforts, spreads risks between development partners, and leverages and scales up existing initiatives that demonstrate results.

New mechanisms should complement what already exists and efforts should be made to join up with successful initiatives supported by other DAC members, particularly when DAC members aim to scale approaches that demonstrate results. New instruments require a number of years to become established and demonstrate results. Working through existing mechanisms offers opportunities to efficiently bring innovations to scale. The African Guarantee Fund[4] is an example of a multilateral private sector engagement instrument that tries to solve the problems of fragmentation, duplication and inefficiencies of development assistance for SMEs in Africa, where several donors and DFIs implement SME programmes in uncoordinated ways, by pooling resources and offering support at the regional level. Working with like-minded DAC members and making use of existing instruments reduces duplication of efforts, spreads risks between development partners, and leverages and scales up existing initiatives that demonstrate results. There are a number of blueprints, tools and innovations on how to work best with the private sector. DAC members can gain efficiencies in the development of new instruments and partnerships by exploring and adopting best practices from other members.

Human resource requirements

Finally, there is a need to consider the human resource implications associated with the use of different private sector engagement mechanisms. More complex engagement mechanisms and partnerships require greater human resources. The increasing number and complexity of products offered to private sector partners require varied staff capacities at headquarters and in embassies. Appropriate capacities are needed for conceptualising, establishing and rolling out new engagement mechanisms. For example, Sida's unit for loans and guarantees is responsible for a guarantee frame of SEK 10 billion (approximately USD 1.17 billion) and plays a critical role in supporting country-level and thematic staff to identify opportunities to use guarantees and in the structuring, implementation and management of guarantees.

The portfolio for private sector engagement

Business-enabling environment

In each reviewed country, private sector representatives stressed that it is critical for DAC members to continue to support the business enabling environment alongside engagement mechanisms. Private sector engagements, regardless of the mechanism used or sector of focus, sit within a broader context in which issues related to regulatory reform, information asymmetries, and market failures undermine possibilities for private investment. Indeed, public support to the private sector is arguably only necessitated by failures within the broader business enabling environment, otherwise the private sector would pursue opportunities on its own. Though direct support is welcome, private sector partners see traditional forms of co-operation by DAC members that support regulatory reform, rule of law and institutional capacity development, among other things, as critical in the context of private sector engagement.

> *It is critical for DAC members to continue to support the business enabling environment alongside engagement mechanisms.*

The mix of private sector engagement mechanisms and how they work together

In terms of the content of private sector engagement portfolios, the use of a range of engagement tools, including financial mechanisms, such as loans, guarantees and grants, and non-financial mechanisms, such as policy dialogue and technical assistance, is an effective way to coherently address development challenges. It is useful to develop a mix of financial and non-financial private sector engagement mechanisms that are flexible and work together. A strategic approach to private sector engagement realises synergies across instruments and approaches. In practice, there are a number of key ways that DAC members can ensure coherence within their portfolios.

One approach is to link support for business-enabling environments with private sector engagement mechanisms. Kindornay and Reilly-King (2013) show that there is a range of opportunities for private sector engagement in the context of private sector development activities.[5] For example, support to policy dialogue on regulatory issues and the promotion of industry standards, including CSR, contributes to a business-enabling environment. In addition to direct investments in countries that support job creation, technology transfer, and domestic resource mobilisation through taxation, the Netherlands partners with the private sector to improve access to finance and enable local businesses to integrate into global value chains. Box 4.3 provides a detailed example of linking private sector engagement activities to private sector development in Ghana.

Box 4.3. **Adopting a range of private sector engagement mechanisms: Denmark and Ghana partner to add value to cashew exports**

Cashew nuts are Ghana's most valuable non-traditional export, with production reaching 68 000 million tonnes in 2015 or around USD 3.5 million in value. Yet up to 95% of Ghana's cashews are exported raw to India, Brazil and Viet Nam for commercial transformation and packaging before being sold on large global consumer markets. This situation is at odds with Ghana's national strategic plan, which highlights the importance of domestic agro-processing for Ghana's economy. The cashew industry has significant potential to contribute to Ghana's development through increased foreign exchange earnings and local processing, which could increase production 20-fold and generate up to 40 000 jobs.

Denmark's approach to supporting Ghana's cashew industry makes use of a range of private sector engagement mechanisms by linking direct business development partnerships to broader reforms aimed at improving the enabling environment for cashew production. In 2013, the Investment Fund for Development, Denmark's DFI, approved a loan of DKK 60.5 million to a joint Danish-Ghanaian company, Mim Cashew, in line with strong growth forecasts for the local processing industry. The loan was intended to support construction of a new factory, enabling the company to double its processing capacity and secure employment for more than 2 000 people in the Bring-Ahafo region. However, by 2015, cashew processing across Ghana had plummeted and most of the country's 13 processing companies had suspended operations. A range of factors were responsible for the turnaround. Over recent years, Ghana experienced an influx of overseas traders receiving concessional interest rates and export subsidies from their home governments. Another problem for Ghanaian-based companies was that local processing incurred a 5% withholding tax on raw nuts, while exporting cashews from Ghana incurred no taxes.

Box 4.3. **Adopting a range of private sector engagement mechanisms: Denmark and Ghana partner to add value to cashew exports** *(continued)*

In late 2015, Ghana's Ministry of Food and Agriculture, together with the African Cashew Initiative and the Danish-supported Business Sector Advocacy Challenge Fund in Ghana, convened a stakeholder workshop to examine potential policy responses to the crisis. To support the discussions, the Business Sector Advocacy Challenge Fund provided evidence-based analysis to help inform Ghana's Ministry of Trade and Industry of recent market developments and put forward a range of options for regulatory reform to support cashew nut processing. Following these consultations, the Ministry of Trade and Industry announced a two-month export window to prohibit export of raw cashews from Ghana in March 2016. The measure aimed to ensure short-term supply of raw cashews for local processing, while continuing to allow overseas traders to purchase and store nuts for export later. However, the directive was revoked just days after it was issued, following concerns that storage facilities for overseas competitors were inadequate and that the bans would result in lower prices for farmers. A broader stakeholder consultation process, initiated by the Ministry of Trade and Industry, is now taking place to build consensus on finding sustainable solutions to Ghana's cashew regulatory challenges and a 10-year cashew development plan is under development.

The example of Danish support for local processing of cashew nuts in Ghana is multifaceted, comprising a range of development co-operation modalities and mechanisms including Investment Fund for Development advisory services, risk capital and loans to aid-funded industry analysis and advocacy support. This example shows the importance of combining private sector engagements with private sector development activities. It demonstrates the potential for development and commercial partners to work together in areas where their objectives overlap. At the same time, it also shows the challenges involved in regulatory reform efforts and the need for buy-in across the value chain in order to achieve sustainable results.

Sources: Republic of Ghana (2014); Macleod and Adu-Mensah (2015), MOFA/ACi/DANIDA (2015), IFU (2014), and "Sustaining the Cashew Industry" (2016).

Non-financial private sector engagement modalities and mechanisms – policy dialogue, sustainable business promotion, and engagements with business associations – are important for laying the groundwork for direct (financial) partnerships with the private sector. Sweden's experience with the Swedish Leadership for Sustainable Development[6] network shows that policy dialogue can be a powerful tool. In this context, Sida has served as a co-ordinator to bring partners (and competitors) together to address social, economic and environmental sustainability issues. The network has built trust among competitors, leading to joint and individual partnerships.

Germany's EZ-Scouts programme[7] seconds development personnel to business associations and has laid the groundwork for direct financial partnerships with the private sector. Also, an important lesson from Germany's experience with responsible business promotion through the creation of hubs in partner countries is that policy dialogue and knowledge sharing activities can be more effective when backed by resources to carry out and scale up activities on the ground.

Another approach to ensuring coherence across private sector engagement portfolios is to integrate responsible business practices directly into engagement mechanisms.

Most DAC members are working to promote CSR, as well as inclusive and responsive business. The Netherlands has found that a useful approach to supporting responsible business conduct – in addition to policy dialogue and participation in standard-setting processes – is to include provisions related to responsible business directly into criteria for partnership. For example, under the Dutch Good Growth Fund, which provides loans to investing and exporting Dutch SMEs and investment funds in partner countries, Dutch applicants must comply with international CSR frameworks and not have tax planning techniques to avoid paying taxes in countries where earnings are generated. Local investment funds must comply with international CSR frameworks, be established in a country with an effective anti-money laundering law, pay taxes in developing countries, be willing to publicly explain and report on its tax policy, and enforce and monitor local clients' (entrepreneurs) compliance with tax laws.

Another approach to ensuring coherence across private sector engagement portfolios is to integrate responsible business practices directly into engagement mechanisms.

For its part, the OECD has been working to promote responsible business conduct (Box 4.4). This work can inform DAC member strategies and approaches toward promoting and harnessing responsible business conduct in development co-operation.

Box 4.4. **OECD efforts to promote responsible business conduct**

In 2015, the OECD developed an action plan to strengthen National Contact Points [on the OECD Guidelines for Multinational Enterprises], focusing on peer reviews, capacity building, peer learning and new tools (OECD, 2016). The action plan reflects the increasing political will to improve and build on the National Contact Points to ensure effective implementation of the OECD guidelines. The OECD is also working on providing more guidance to businesses on how to implement the recommendations of the OECD guidelines and is working to promote responsible business conduct more broadly with partner countries that do not formally adhere to them.

Excerpt from: Bule, T. and C. Tebar Less (2016), "Promoting sustainable development through responsible business conduct", Development Co-operation Report 2016: The Sustainable Development Goals as Business Opportunities, OECD Publishing, Paris, http://dx.doi.org/10.1787/dcr-2016-en, p.133.

Flexibility in implementation and the roles of headquarters and field staff

Country reviews also consistently highlighted the importance of flexibility in the use of engagement mechanisms. Adapting mechanisms to the needs of partners ensures that mechanisms are fit for purpose and can maximise the impact of partnership. The selection of private sector mechanisms should be grounded in development priorities and a thorough analysis of local opportunities and constraints. In this way, the selection of mechanisms can be grounded in an explicit understanding of what DAC members are trying to achieve and how specific mechanisms can contribute to success. Providing country-level staff with flexibility and authority to select mechanisms and private sector partners is important for ensuring that activities and partnerships are efficiently carried out at country level and grounded in local realities and priorities. Sweden's experience in Zambia highlights[8] how private sector engagement mechanisms can be effectively linked and adapted to a country context. The embassy team made use of a business development facility, multi-stakeholder partnerships with business, government and civil society, technical assistance, a guarantee and a partnership with civil society to contribute to the overall objective of supporting economic growth and development.

The selection of private sector mechanisms should be grounded in development priorities and a thorough analysis of local opportunities and constraints.

Overall, there is a need to balance the origination of private sector engagements between headquarter and field levels across private sector engagement portfolios. DAC members' mechanisms to engage the private sector are implemented with varying degrees of decentralisation. For some members the bulk of private sector engagements are developed at the headquarter level, whereas for others field staff are responsible for originating partnerships. There is a need to balance these two approaches as both are characterised by opportunities and challenges. It can be challenging to ensure that initiatives which originate at headquarters have sufficient buy-in at the country level. Yet, some forms of private sector engagement require a centralised approach and headquarter leadership, such as global initiatives aimed at policy dialogue with the private sector on standard setting.

Evolution and continuity of private sector engagement mechanisms

Finally, reviewed countries highlighted the importance of experimentation and reflection on the effectiveness of private sector engagement mechanisms. They noted the need to allow time to test new mechanisms, experiment and engage in an iterative process. This approach allows for evaluation, learning and the evolution of portfolios and approaches and helps to ensure that mechanisms are fit for purpose.

As portfolios evolve, however, it is important to consider continuity. Private sector partners plan their strategies around the mechanisms that have been established by governments. As such, a certain amount of predictability is appreciated by partners as a means to reduce their risks when exploring strategies for engagement with government.

Notes

1. For more information, see: www.oecd.org/dac/peer-reviews/Private-Sector-Engagement-Terminology-and-Typology.pdf.
2. For more information, see: www.oecd.org/dac/peer-reviews/develoPPP-de.pdf.
3. For more information, see: www.oecd.org/dac/peer-reviews/Overseas-Private-Investment-Corporation.pdf.
4. For more information, see: www.oecd.org/dac/peer-reviews/African-Guarantee-Fund.pdf.
5. See Miyamoto and Chiofalo (2016) for an overview of donor support to private sector development activities more generally.
6. For more information, see: www.oecd.org/dac/peer-reviews/Swedish-Leadership-for-Sustainable-Development.pdf.
7. For more information, see: www.oecd.org/dac/peer-reviews/Agency-for-Business-and-Economic-Development-and-EZ-Scouts.pdf.
8. For more information, see: www.oecd.org/dac/peer-reviews/Swedish-International-Development-Cooperation-Agency.pdf.

References

Benn, J. et al. (2016), "Amounts mobilised from the private sector by official development finance interventions: Guarantees, syndicated loans and shares in collective investment vehicles", *OECD Development Co-operation Working Papers*, No. 26, OECD Publishing, Paris, http://dx.doi.org/10.1787/5jm3xh459n37-en.

Bilal, S. et al. (2014), "De-coding Public-Private Partnerships for Development", *ECDPM Discussion Paper*, No. 161, European Centre for Development Policy Management, Maastricht, http://ecdpm.org/wp-content/uploads/DP-161_Decoding-Public-Private-Partnerships-Development-2014.pdf.

BMZ (2011), "Forms of development cooperation involving the private sector", *Strategy paper*, No. 05/2011e, Federal Ministry for Economic Cooperation and Development, Bonn and Berlin, www.bmz.de/en/publications/archiv/type_of_publication/strategies/Strategiepapier306_05_2011.pdf.

Bule, T. and C. Tebar Less (2016), "Promoting sustainable development through responsible business conduct", *Development Co-operation Report 2016: The Sustainable Development Goals as Business Opportunities*, OECD Publishing, Paris, http://dx.doi.org/10.1787/dcr-2016-en.

Byiers, B. and A. Rosengren (2012), "Common or conflicting interests? Reflections on the private sector (for) development agenda", *Discussion Paper*, No. 131, European Centre for Development Policy Management, Maastricht, http://ecdpm.org/wp-content/uploads/2013/11/DP-131-Conflicting-Interests-Private-Sector-Development-Agenda-2012.pdf.

Di Bella, J. et al. (2013), "Mapping private sector engagements in development cooperation, The North-South Institute, Ottawa, www.nsi-ins.ca/publications/mapping-private-sector-engagements-in-development-cooperation.

IFU (2014), "Annual report 2014", Investment Fund for Developing Countries, Copenhagen, www.ifu.dk/dk/materiale/pdf-filer/ifu-annual-report-2014.

Kindornay, S. and F. Reilly-King (2013), "Investing in the business of development: Bilateral donor approaches to engaging the private sector", The North-South Institute and Canadian Council for International Co-operation, Ottawa, www.nsi-ins.ca/publications/investing-in-the-business-of-development.

MacLeod, J. and K. Adu-Mensah (2015), "Options for processor support: Analysis of raw cashew nut trade measures", Cashew stakeholders meeting presentation.

Miyamoto, K. and E. Chiofalo (2016), "Development co-operation for private sector development: Analytical framework and measuring official development finance", DCD/DAC/AGID(2016)1/REV1, OECD Publishing, Paris, www.oecd.org/officialdocuments/publicdisplaydocumentpdf/?cote=DCD/DAC/AGID(2016)1/REV1&docLanguage=En.

OECD (2016). *Action Plan for National Contact Points for the OECD Guidelines for Multinational Enterprises*, OECD, Paris, http://mneguidelines.oecd.org/ncps.

Chapter 5

Partnering for sustainable development

This chapter provides lessons for partnering with different stakeholders in private sector engagements and identifies factors that contribute to successful partnerships. An important overarching message is that the selection of partners in development co-operation should be determined by development objectives and desired results. Depending on goals, partner country governments, CSOs, multilateral organisations, the private sector or a combination of stakeholders may be best placed to realise results. It is helpful to use diverse approaches to private sector engagement that offer opportunities to a range of different types of private sector actors in line with the goals of development co-operation. The chapter also provides lessons on the inclusion of traditional development partners, such as knowledge institutions, CSOs and multilateral organisations, in private sector engagements. The final section of the chapter focuses on lessons for successful partnership. It highlights the need to develop effective mechanisms to attract the right partners, include provisions for scaling success into the initial design of partnerships, ensure alignment of interests, and be inclusive in multi-stakeholder partnerships.

Establishing successful cross-sector partnerships

The increasing focus on private sector engagements and multi-stakeholder partnerships in development co-operation has been accompanied by research and policy papers on how to best collaborate across sectors. DAC members and other development partners have identified lessons from their experiences with private sector partnerships (Ministry of Foreign Affairs of the Netherlands, 2010; Pfisterer, 2013) and supported various initiatives that promote cross-sector partnerships, carry out research and analysis, and develop tools for effective partnering, such as the Partnering Initiative, Partnerships Resource Centre and Practitioner Hub for Inclusive Business.[1] Reviews of private sector collaborations and partnerships have given rise to a range of best practices and emerging lessons (Garside et al., 2016; Development Initiatives, 2015; Kindornay, Tissot and Sheiban, 2014; Kindornay, Higgins and Olender, 2013; McKinsey & Company, 2009; Partnerships Resource Centre, 2013; Pattberg and Widerberg, 2014; PPPLab, 2014a). Reviews have noted the importance of: aligned interests and clear objectives; contributions beyond finance from partners to realise the full value of working across sectors; clearly defined roles and responsibilities; harnessing comparative advantages and differences between partners; mutual benefits for all partners; and clear ground rules as well as possibilities for partnerships to evolve and adapt over time.

The lessons arising from the academic and policy literature resonate with those emerging from the peer learning review. The following sections outline lessons pertaining to partners and partnerships.

Partners

The literature on working across sectors is clear on the need to ensure that partnerships are rooted in shared interests and a clear understanding of objectives. In this sense, the choice of partner depends on each party's overall objectives and the alignment between them. In the case of private sector engagements for development, the overarching objective of ODA is realising development results. The Sustainable Development Goals offer an important framework in terms of identifying development results in this regard. Development objectives and desired results should determine the selection of partners. In some instances, the private sector is best placed to contribute to results while in others it is partner governments, non-governmental organisations, knowledge institutions, multilateral organisations or a combination of partners. The decision to partner with the private sector should be rooted in a theory of change that establishes whether and how the private sector is best placed to help realise specific development results. This approach ensures that development objectives are central to partner selection processes, even when combined with other objectives such as promoting commercial interests.

> *Development objectives and desired results should determine the selection of partners.*

The importance of focusing on development objectives is also particularly important given the trade-offs that government institutions often face when selecting investments to support. As noted above, the general rule is that government and private sector actors should work together when it is clear that shared value can be realised – better development outcomes from profitable business and investments. However, in practice, there can be and are real trade-offs between development and for-profit objectives. For example, investments that focus on the middle class, rather than the base of the pyramid, are typically more attractive to the private sector in terms of risk and return. This issue becomes particularly challenging in a context characterised by a lack of bankable projects and organisations facing pressure to spend funds within particular time periods, with particular partners or to realise certain rates of return.[2] Making desired development results the starting point in decision-making processes is a helpful way to guide the selection of potential private sector partners and investments.

Partner countries

A number of studies have questioned the extent to which private sector engagements in development co-operation sufficiently include partner country governments, or at the very least support national development plans and priorities (Kindornay and Reilly-King, 2013; Crishna Morgado et al., forthcoming; World Economic Forum and OECD, 2015; Bilal et al., 2014). Crishna Morgado et al. (forthcoming) conclude that there is a need for stronger links with national development plans and priorities based on a review of private sector engagements in the area of environmental sustainability and climate change. They note that ensuring national ownership is important for overall development effectiveness and for longer-term scaling up of successful projects. At a 2015 workshop on blended finance held by the World Economic Forum and OECD, participants also highlighted the need to promote local ownership of blended finance investments (World Economic Forum and OECD, 2015). To achieve this, they suggested allocating finance to investments that are part of national strategies, supporting capacity development of local investment entities and working with partner countries on the regulatory environment to promote blended finance. Bilal et al. (2014) argue that future partnerships must build on partner countries' own strategies to finance sustainable development and be better linked to nationally owned development agendas.

Partner country governments should be included in country-level private sector engagement activities.

The limited emphasis on aid effectiveness principles in DAC members' private sector engagement policies suggests that the concerns outlined above likely remain valid. Moreover, the use of centralised, demand-driven private sector engagement mechanisms also raises the question of how partner countries are brought into private sector engagements. Nevertheless, the peer learning review showed that DAC members are including partner country governments in private sector engagement activities. For example, Sweden's approach in Zambia highlights[3] initiatives that include the local government, the Millennium Challenge Corporation's Public-Private Partnership Platform[4] aims to build partner country capacity to carry out PPPs, and Box 4.3 provides an example of Denmark's efforts to support Ghana's policy priorities through private sector engagement. Reviewed countries also highlighted that partner country governments should be included in country-level private sector engagement activities, at the very least in terms of providing perspectives and direction on activities. This approach is critical for ownership and local buy-in, as well as building country-level capacity to engage with the private sector.

The role of DAC members: The public offer

DAC members play a number of important roles in the context of private sector engagements. They provide finance, expertise and access to local networks, act as facilitators of multi-stakeholder partnerships and discussions, and promote responsible business, among other things (see e.g. Di Bella et al., 2013; Kindornay, Higgins and Olender, 2013; Bilal et al., 2014; PPPLab, 2014b). In addition to what they can provide, DAC members have legitimacy and credibility in development co-operation that makes them desirable partners for the private sector and others.

The peer learning review supports what is already known in the academic and policy literature. When engaging the private sector, DAC members should rely on their comparative advantages and be clear about what government offers. Financial mechanisms are critical for private sector engagement and DAC members can play a number of important roles to harness private sector finance. In the area of innovative financing, government can aggregate investments, blend concessionary and non-concessionary finance, and co-ordinate with the private sector.[5] Government partners can aggregate multiple investments – which individually may not be appealing to investors – to attract institutional investors and create a diversified risk profile. They can also blend concessionary and non-concessionary finance to encourage investments and diminish risks. For example, the Currency Exchange Fund[6] develops markets for long-term exchange rate risk and interest rate risk hedging products in partner countries where such markets do not yet exist. The provision of risk capital by Germany and the Netherlands has facilitated participation by another 22 investors and led to hedging of USD 1.5 billion in loans to borrowers in partner countries, particularly benefiting microfinance institutions and SMEs, since 2007. Finally, government can bring private sector actors into development finance discussions and co-ordinate with them to bring instruments to market. For example, Convergence and the Sustainable Development Investment Partnership are examples of initiatives that aim to improve co-ordination among investors to promote investment in partner countries.[7]

Non-financial contributions are equally important. Government institutions offer valuable expertise, on-the-ground knowledge, and experience and networks in partner countries. The focus on cross-cutting issues such as gender, human rights, the environment and anti-corruption is part of the value added that government (and implementing partners) bring to partnerships with the private sector. Notwithstanding efforts by the private sector to promote greater social, economic and environmental sustainability in their business operations, the review showed that private sector partners value the expertise that development partners and DFIs bring to collaboration. The integration of cross-cutting issues into projects is an important way to anchor partnerships and demonstrate how private sector engagement realises development results. DAC members' in-country presence is also appreciated by private sector partners because it provides them with a contact point in case issues arise over the course of private sector engagements as well as a source of expertise and networking.

With the establishment of private sector engagement mechanisms, DAC members should focus on their areas of comparative advantage as a starting point and be clear about what they offer to potential partners. This approach is particularly important given that even with specific expertise, new mechanisms are likely to require new capacities that may or may not exist in-house, as noted in Chapters 2 and 4. Working in areas where expertise already exists is one way to mitigate this challenge and demonstrate the added value of government partners.

Private sector

Companies

The possibilities for private sector engagement differ according to the results sought in development co-operation and the capacities of different private sector partners. As Heinrich (2015) points out, SMEs tend to require additional support in terms of technical advice and management to succeed. In comparison to larger companies, SMEs usually have more limited capacities and require access to simple financial instruments (Garside et al., 2016). Experience from the Netherlands also suggests that SMEs require greater support to meet partnership requirements, particularly in terms of CSR requirements. For SMEs domiciled in developing countries, these challenges can be exacerbated by issues such as informality and weak legal and regulatory systems. Yet, local SMEs also often have greater knowledge of local development challenges and potential solutions. In addition, SMEs in partner countries and DAC member countries often face greater financing gaps than larger companies and have a special need for government support.

Multinational companies and larger companies domiciled in partner countries have greater capacity and are often able to meet partnership requirements more easily than SMEs. Moreover, they tend to have greater capacity to implement projects and contribute to large-scale and systematic development impacts (Heinrich, 2015). As with the case of local SMEs, large companies in partner countries face similar challenges to those noted above. In general, it can be more difficult to demonstrate financial additionality for larger companies than in the case of SMEs.

The peer learning review identified a number of ways that DAC members can address the needs of different private sector partners. For SMEs, reviewed countries are making use of streamlined application processes as well as the provision of mixed modalities that support the adoption of good CSR practices, feasibility studies and capacity development to effectively engage in development co-operation (Box 5.1). It is also important to consider a phased financing approach for SMEs. As noted in Chapter 4, SMEs are often able to access grant and other forms of start-up financing, but face a financing gap before they are eligible to apply for larger financing windows. This was a key lesson for Sweden from its experience with its Innovations Against Poverty challenge fund, which provided small grants to start-ups and SMEs. Sweden is now exploring ways to address this financing gap.

With respect to larger companies, and in particular multinational companies, the review revealed that some DAC members are moving from project-based relationships to more strategic forms of engagement rooted in memoranda of understanding. The Netherlands and the United States have developed agreements with multinational companies that outline provisions for private sector collaboration and partnerships. This approach is helpful for managing relationships with larger companies that include a range of projects. The United States has also established a Relationship Managers Network at

USAID. The network provides dedicated contact points to key corporate and philanthropic partners and aims to build trust between USAID and partner companies. This approach also ensures coherence in USAID's overall approach to engagement since relationship managers have a bird's-eye view of the multiple projects and initiatives in which each private sector partner is engaged.

Different types of private sector partners require different types of engagement.

Different types of private sector partners require different types of engagement. Offering a range of mechanisms that recognise the different needs and capacities of private sector actors is an important way to facilitate engagement with a diverse range of private sector partners.

Box 5.1. **Making finance more accessible to SMEs: OPIC's experience with impact investing**

Since 2008, OPIC, the United States' DFI, has been developing a suite of private sector instruments to support impact investing. In this context, OPIC recognised that SMEs, in particular, were unable to access financing owing to OPIC's demanding application process. To address this issue, OPIC developed a range of streamlined financial mechanisms. OPIC's Portfolio for Impact programme provides financing, under modified criteria and with a higher risk threshold, to projects that are small or nascent. The Innovative Financial Intermediaries Program provides funding for smaller-scale financial intermediaries and investment vehicles with a variety of structures. To qualify for impact investing tools, applicants must submit a business plan, a financial model, a feasibility, marketing and sector study, an environmental assessment, and financial statements that demonstrate a history of sound management practices. In addition, proposed projects much include the aspects of additionality and ownership as well as capitalisation or leverage of 50%. The Enterprise Development Network helps SMEs seeking funding or technical assistance to develop funding application packages, refine marketing strategies, and draft or enhance their business plans.

Source: www.oecd.org/dac/peer-reviews/Overseas-Private-Investment-Corporation.pdf.

Chambers of commerce and business associations

In the literature on private sector engagement in development co-operation, much of the focus is on companies in the private sector with relatively little attention paid to business associations. An assessment of private sector engagement mechanisms across DAC members indicates that, if featured at all, most business associations and chambers of commerce are not targeted for direct partnership programmes, but rather engagement in policy dialogue.

A key feature of Germany's engagement with the private sector that stands out in relation to other DAC members is its emphasis on chambers of commerce and business associations. Germany works with business membership organisations to convene businesses for policy dialogue and provide information on engagement opportunities and investment opportunities in partner countries. Importantly, Germany also carries out direct partnerships with business membership organisations in the provision of technical and vocational education and training, as well as to support the establishment of similar organisations in developing countries (see Chambers and Associations Partnership Programme [KVP] and Vocational Education and Training Partnership Programme [BBP])[8]. Through this approach, Germany is able to reach a wide range of potential partners, promote knowledge sharing given its extensive domestic experience in establishing business membership organisations, and support businesses in partner countries to organise and engage with local government. The German experience shows that chambers of commerce and business associations are important partners in private sector engagements and may serve as untapped partners for many DAC members in their private sector engagement strategies.

Chambers of commerce and business associations are important partners in private sector engagements.

Other development partners

Foundations and private philanthropy

Given the focus of the peer learning review on the for-profit sector, less attention was paid to the role of foundations and private philanthropy in discussions. There is no doubt that philanthropy is playing a greater role in development co-operation, with foundations serving as important partners for DAC members. Foundations play a role in mobilising financial resources and have flexibility in their operations, capacity for innovation and risk taking, and valuable knowledge and expertise (Missika and Romon, 2014). An assessment of DAC members' private sector engagement policies reveals very little mention (if any at all) of private philanthropy and foundations as partners. Nevertheless, in practice many DAC members are working with foundations, such as the Bill & Melinda Gates Foundation, in multi-stakeholder partnerships with the private sector (see e.g. partnership profiles[9] and Kindornay, Higgins and Olender [2013] for specific initiatives). The role of private philanthropy was highlighted by staff during the country review of the United States. Staff noted that while it is important to focus on core business in private sector engagements, private philanthropy continues to play a critical role in supporting development initiatives. Going forward, DAC members can further engage with foundations by drawing on comparative advantages to leverage finance and impact, as well as through participation in formal partnerships (Missika and Ramon, 2014).

Knowledge partners

Universities and research institutions are important partners in private sector engagements. The country reviews on the Netherlands and the United States, in particular, noted the value of knowledge partners in conducting research and developing innovations that can be taken to market or used to inform private sector engagement activities. The Netherlands supports knowledge partners to carry out research on effective partnerships and assess the impacts of private sector engagements (Box 5.2). In the Netherlands' experience, working with independent knowledge partners ensures that activities are informed by the latest research and lends additional credibility to discussions on the effectiveness and impacts of private sector engagements. The US Feed the Future initiative[10] allocates 15% of resources to universities that contribute through research and development. Innovations developed by universities can then be tested and scaled, as appropriate, by implementing partners.

Box 5.2. **Assessing the effectiveness of private sector engagements: The PPPLab**

In 2014, the Dutch government provided support to the PPPLab, a four-year initiative, to improve the relevance, effectiveness and quality of PPPs as targeted instruments in Dutch international co-operation in the areas of water and food security and private sector development. The PPPLab is implemented by a consortium of knowledge partners comprised of the Partnerships Resource Centre, Aqua for All, Centre for Development Innovation at Wageningen University and Research Centre, and SNV Netherlands Development Organisation. It works in close co-operation with the Sustainable Water Fund and Facility for Sustainable Entrepreneurship and Food Security and co-ordinates activities with VIA Water, a knowledge platform for the Dutch water sector, and the Food & Business Knowledge Platform.

The PPPLab's overarching research and learning questions are: how do PPPs contribute to the realisation of Dutch policy goals regarding water and food security and private sector development? What challenges are met and what successes are achieved? What (potential) improvements can thus be identified? To address these questions, the PPPLab examines four key areas: 1) business models, with the focus being the development of an analytical tool and broader application to strengthen business sustainability and improve understanding of various partnership business models; 2) scaling up and system change, specifically scaling up outcomes of and system change resulting from individual PPPs; 3) governance and government, providing insight into partnership governance (e.g. partners' identities, roles and contributions including the ways they work together) and the public sector's role within PPPs (e.g. engagement by local public entities); and 4) partnership performance tracking, particularly monitoring processes that partnerships can use to track how they are performing as partnerships and study the correlation between how a partnership functions and how well it delivers outcomes.

Source: www.oecd.org/dac/peer-reviews/PPPlab.pdf.

Civil society organisations

CSOs bring value to private sector engagements as representatives of specific communities or issue areas, watchdogs, experts and implementing partners (PPPLab, 2014b; Kindornay, Higgins and Olender, 2013). In their private sector engagements, DAC members are supporting multi-stakeholder initiatives with CSOs, including policy dialogue and partnerships, allocating funding to CSOs to implement projects in partnership with companies and provide capacity development to local businesses, including to local co-operatives and SMEs, and providing support for CSOs to carry out their watchdog function and hold companies and governments to account (Box 5.3). CSOs are also active in the field of social business and entrepreneurship.

> *Though CSOs and private sector actors are already co-operating in development, the provision of dedicated funds for multi-stakeholder partnerships has potential to further facilitate such partnerships.*

The review revealed the importance of respecting the role of CSOs and ensuring that space in terms of policy dialogue and funding exists to facilitate CSO engagement in addressing complex development challenges alongside the private sector and government. Though CSOs and private sector actors are already co-operating in development, the provision of dedicated funds for multi-stakeholder partnerships has potential to further facilitate such partnerships.

In addition, the review showed that CSOs often require resources to effectively partner with the private sector in development. Development partners play an important role in terms of convening partnerships. They can also support CSOs to develop projects

Box 5.3. Supporting CSOs in private sector engagements: Sweden's Drivers of Change progamme

Sida's Drivers of Change programme works to influence the private sector to operate in more sustainable and inclusive ways and thereby contribute to poverty reduction. The programme is grounded in a recognition of the importance of civil society as an advocate for responsible business conduct and a watchdog with respect to the negative impacts of business operations on development outcomes. A Driver of Change is an organisation or change agent that works to influence the private sector or the market for the benefit of people living in poverty and for sustainable development. The programme targets sector reforms rather than individual companies. It supports advocacy efforts as well as CSO-led partnerships with the private sector. The types of initiatives supported by the programme include civil society advocacy and partnerships around issues such as labour standards, environmental problems and anti-corruption. A Driver of Change can be based in any country, but the effects of its activities must have a large impact on people living in poverty in low-income countries.

An example of a Driver of Change project is Sida's support for Swedwatch. Swedwatch is an initiative that seeks to minimise the negative footprint of businesses with the aim of contributing to poverty reduction and sustainability, as well as a positive impact on the private sector through research connected to human rights and the environment. In its watchdog role, Swedwatch monitors human rights and serves as a whistleblower, pushing companies to act in accordance with international standards. The initiative also includes the sharing of best practices with the aim of raising the bar for CSR. Swedwatch produces reports on the impacts of companies that it investigates and consumers.

Sources: Sida (23 May 2014a), "Collaboration opportunities: Drivers of Change", www.sida.se/English/partners/our-partners/Private-sector/Collaboration-opportunities/Drivers-of-Change; Sida (2012c), "The watchdog, whistleblower and lantern", Swedish International Development Cooperation Agency, Stockholm, www.sida.se/English/where-we-work/Asia/Bangladesh/examples-of-results/The-Watchdog-Whistleblower-and-Lantern (accessed 11 July 2016).

and dialogue platforms with the private sector. The process of co-creating projects with the private sector is typically resource intensive. Many non-profit partners do not have a budget from which they can draw to participate in project development and, as such, require additional support in early stages.

Multilateral development institutions

Finally, DAC members are working with multilateral development institutions in the area of private sector engagement. As with the case of CSOs, DAC members allocate funds to the United Nations and other multilateral institutions to implement projects in partnership with the private sector. They are also supporting multilateral policy dialogues and standard-setting initiatives such as the United Nations Global Compact and the Business Call to Action network.[11] Finally, DAC members are working with and through multilateral institutions to leverage private sector finance through, for example, specialised funds and initiatives such as the Sustainable Development Investment Partnership.[12] Participation in multilateral efforts is an effective way to engage the private sector because it facilitates greater risk-sharing among donors and economies of scale.

As with the case of CSOs, multilateral institutions are often unable to fully engage in co-creation processes with the private sector without dedicated funds when serving as an implementing partner. This situation can undermine their ability to engage effectively in partnerships once they are formally established because of the lack of initial engagement and input when setting up a partnership.

Partnerships

Attract the right partners

If you build it, the private sector may not come. DAC members have learned the importance of dedicating resources to attracting the right partners for private sector engagements. The review reveals at least three ways that DAC members can attract the right partners.

First, clearly communicate private sector engagement opportunities and entry points. To facilitate engagement, potential private sector partners should be able to easily identify possible opportunities, assess if they align with their interests and have a clear understanding of how to contact aid agencies for follow-up. Through its Global Development Alliances programme, the United States makes use of an annual programme statement that outlines priority areas for partnership. Germany has established an Agency for Business and Economic Development that provides information and advice to companies seeking to partner with the German government in development co-operation.[13]

Second, effective marketing is important for ensuring that partners understand engagement mechanisms, requirements and desired results. In this context, speaking the language of the private sector also matters. For example, using terminology such as emerging markets rather than referring to particular regions can be more attractive to potential investors. Rather than referring to log-frames and results-based frameworks, it may be more effective to speak in terms of milestones.

Actively promote private sector engagement opportunities.

Finally, in addition to providing an entry point for potential partners and clearly communicating opportunities with terminology that private sector partners will understand, it is important to actively promote private sector engagement opportunities. The secondment of development professionals to private chambers of commerce and business associations through Germany's EZ-Scouts programme,[14] for instance, is an important means to increase private sector engagement. Policy dialogue with the private sector on key opportunities is also helpful.

Know the end game

Reviewed countries also highlighted the need to identify desired systemic changes from the outset during the establishment of projects and partnerships (see also Kindornay, Higgins and Olender, 2013). This approach is important at both project and instrument levels. At the project level, consideration for how pilots will be scaled later if successful is important. At the mechanism level, private sector instruments that provide grant funding may need to be linked to less concessional financing schemes or provide support to partners to access commercial financing once the grant has ended, as highlighted in Chapter 4. Without consideration for scale and broader systemic changes during design phases, it can be difficult to move past one-off partnerships or innovations to larger-scale approaches.

Ensure interests align

As mentioned, a clear lesson from assessments of private sector partnerships is that interests must align for them to be successful, with all parties understanding objectives and how a partnership contributes to realising individual and shared value. In practice, reviewed countries noted that shared value can be realised by working with private sector partners that have an incentive to ensure the long-term sustainability of projects and initiatives. Often this approach involves focusing on core business activities in private sector engagements. For example, the United States works with private sector partners whose core business aligns with the US government's development objectives. The United States sees this approach as critical to ensuring sustainability – private sector partners should have a real (profit-making) stake in the outcomes of the partnerships in which they engage. Reviewed countries also found that local companies are equally important partners from a sustainability perspective. Domestic companies will often continue to operate in countries, whereas foreign investors are sometimes more likely to leave when country-level circumstances change. Overall, private sector engagements should aim to produce "more and better" business over the long term (Box 5.4).

Box 5.4. **What is more and better business?**

The International Dialogue on Peacebuilding and Statebuilding and BNP Paribas Investment Partners (forthcoming) set out a useful way to understand the promotion of more and better business in fragile and conflict-affected states that can be broadened to apply to all partner countries. More business refers to greater volumes of domestic and foreign private investment in businesses in partner countries. Better business means investment that complies with international standards for responsible business conduct, avoids doing harm and takes a proactive approach to contributing to development results.

Multi-stakeholder partnerships

Inclusivity and engaging a range of stakeholders

As mentioned, partner country governments, CSOs and knowledge institutions have valuable contributions to make to private sector engagements. Complex challenges often require complex solutions with involvement by a wide variety of stakeholders. Partner country perspectives are key to ensuring ownership and buy-in. Civil society is an important implementing partner and watchdog. Involvement by civil society helps to ensure transparency and accountability in multi-stakeholder partnerships and can lend greater legitimacy to initiatives by ensuring that they are grounded in the perspectives and interests of beneficiaries. Finally, the knowledge institutions have a role in developing testable innovations and can support evaluation of partnerships and their outcomes. Figure 5.1 provides an overview of the Dutch approach to multi-stakeholder initiatives and highlights the contributions that different stakeholders make and the benefits that they incur.

Figure 5.1. **The "Dutch Diamond Approach" to sustainable development**

Government	Private sector	Knowledge partners	Civil society
Leverages: Finance, convening power, networks and expertise	Leverages: Finance, technical expertise and innovative approaches	Leverage: Knowledge, expertise and applied reseach capacity	Leverages: Expertise, local networks and reputation
Benefits: Scale, finance, expertise and innovative approaches	Benefits: Knowledge, expertise, networks, funding and market access	Benefits: Research opportunities, including learning from partnerships	Benefits: Extended influence, funding, expertise and new approaches

Source: Government of the Netherlands (n.d.), "Public-private partnerships", www.government.nl/topics/development-cooperation/contents/development-cooperation-partners-and-partnerships/public-private-partnerships (accessed 1 July 2016).

Reviewed countries learned that it is important to be inclusive of all relevant stakeholders from the beginning and prepared to compromise. Willingness to compromise and build flexibility into partnership structures to meet the needs of all partners is important. All participants should be included in decision-making processes with members making decisions and moving forward on them together. This approach helps to build trust among participants and ensures continued buy-in from participants. However, to enable members to move forward together, partners often need to adjust their expectations at times to ensure that all actors are able to come on board.

Successful multi-stakeholder partnerships

In launching multi-stakeholder partnerships, it is important to know how and what can be negotiated when partnering with the private sector. Rather than allowing discussions to circle around ideas, DAC members should be prepared to put next steps on the table and cut ties when it is clear that a partnership is not going to work.

> *Partnerships work best when based on shared value, shared interests, clear roles and responsibilities, comparative advantages, risks and rewards.*

In the event that a partnership can go forward, DAC members have found that partnerships work best when based on shared value, shared interests, clear roles and responsibilities, comparative advantages, risks and rewards. The experiences of DAC members indeed resonate with the success factors that have been identified by others when working through multi-stakeholder partnerships. It is important to understand the goals and needs of each partner, focus on value addition from the outset, and establish clear roles and expectations, including with respect to how decision-making processes will occur. In this context, establishing common terminology in multi-stakeholder partnerships can be a challenge. Partners undergo a learning curve in this regard and in some respects must understand the terminologies of business, government and civil society.[15]

In addition, solid commitments by partners in multi-stakeholder partnerships are important to ensure that all partners are fully dedicated to an initiative. Commitments do not always need to be financial – they can come in the form of in-kind contributions. Regardless of the nature of commitments, all partners should be willing to put resources into the initiative.

Finally, the review also pointed to the need for DAC members to see partnerships as a relationship and not a contract. The growth and expansion of new partnerships require maintenance of relationships. The soft skills noted in Chapter 2 are of critical importance to build trust with potential partners and engage more easily in exchanges on potential projects and work through co-creation processes.

The innovative and nimble government partner

Development co-operation works at a different pace than the private sector. On the one hand, government institutions need to be positioned to harness opportunities quickly. This approach involves ensuring that tools and processes are structured to enable staff to move quickly when opportunities arise. Bureaucratic processes can be a challenge for private sector partners and DAC members facilitating engagement processes. On the other hand, it is important to also be patient and wait for good opportunities rather than rush into partnerships. Good analysis of challenges and possible solutions, which takes time, is important for identifying opportunities.

Create spaces that encourage individuals to innovate and work together to find solutions to complex challenges.

DAC members also facilitate opportunities. They can create spaces that encourage individuals to innovate and work together to find solutions to complex challenges. Germany makes use of the Lab of Tomorrow to bring together private sector stakeholders and others to identify solutions to development challenges (GIZ, 2016). The Lab uses unique buildings and spaces to bring participants together to brainstorm potential business models to address challenges. GIZ, which implements the Lab, identifies challenges, but leaves it up to private sector partners to identify the solutions. Solutions are then backed up with financial and technical assistance commitments by GIZ for further development.

Among other approaches, USAID uses its Broad Agency Announcements to collaborate and promote innovation with the private sector and other organisations to address development challenges without clearly defined solutions. Under this approach, the private sector is invited to submit solutions to development challenges. The approach encourages private sector partners to co-define problems and co-create solutions with government, including through the use of systems thinking.

There is no one way to organise the interface between government and the private sector. There is a need to balance strict procedures and autonomy in private sector engagements. Though strict procedures autonomy are not mutually exclusive, too much autonomy may make it difficult for government institutions to engage companies without a clear focus. Yet, a structure that allows freedom for mistakes and experimentation with projects promotes innovation.

Moreover, not all challenges require new structures and initiatives. DAC members can harness existing partnerships, facilities and networks to promote innovation. This approach is particularly important in resource-constrained contexts. Rather than launching new partnerships and initiatives as a first response to development challenges, DAC members should look to what already exists globally and at the local level as a means to reduce duplication of efforts and harness existing momentum toward sustainable solutions.

Finally, internationalise success when an initiative works. Take country-level initiatives to the international level where possible to broaden the scope of partnership. Broadening multi-stakeholder partnerships from the country level to the regional or global levels can be an important way to scale up successful initiatives. This approach can also serve as part of an exit strategy for government. As initiatives grow, membership fees and other payment structures can be used to sustain them.

Notes

1. See http://thepartneringinitiative.org, www.rsm.nl/prc and www.inclusivebusinesshub.org, respectively.
2. In particular, DFIs have been highly criticised by civil society on this latter point. See, for instance, Romero (2014) and Kwakkenbos (2012).
3. For more information, see: www.oecd.org/dac/peer-reviews/Swedish-International-Development-Cooperation-Agency.pdf.
4. For more information, see: www.oecd.org/dac/peer-reviews/Public-Private-Partnership-Platform.pdf.
5. See Guarnaschelli et al. (2014) for a full discussion of innovative financing.
6. For more information, see: www.oecd.org/dac/peer-reviews/Currency-Exchange-Fund.pdf.
7. See https://convergence.finance and www.sdiponline.org.
8. For more information, see: www.oecd.org/dac/peer-reviews/Chambers-Associations-Partnership-Programme.pdf and www.oecd.org/dac/peer-reviews/Vocational-Education-and-Training-Partnership-Programme.pdf.
9. For more information, see For the full suite of private sector peer learning outputs, see: www.oecd.org/dac/peer-reviews/private-sector-engagement-for-sustainable-development-lessons-from-the-dac.htm.
10. For more information, see: www.oecd.org/dac/peer-reviews/Feed-the-Future.pdf.
11. See www.unglobalcompact.org and www.businesscalltoaction.org, respectively.
12. See www.sdiponline.org.
13. See www.bmz.de/webapps/wirtschaft/#/de.
14. For more information, see: www.oecd.org/dac/peer-reviews/Agency-for-Business-and-Economic-Development-and-EZ-Scouts.pdf.
15. Kindornay, Higgins and Olender (2013) had a similar finding in their review of trade-related private sector partnerships.

References

Bilal, S. et al. (2014), "De-coding Public-Private Partnerships for Development", *ECDPM Discussion Paper*, No. 161, European Centre for Development Policy Management, Maastricht, http://ecdpm.org/wp-content/uploads/DP-161_Decoding-Public-Private-Partnerships-Development-2014.pdf.

Crishna Morgado, N. et al. (forthcoming), "Development co-operation and private sector engagement for the environment – a scoping paper", OECD Publishing, Paris.

Development Initiatives (2015), "The role of the private sector in development effectiveness: Common components of success in future partnerships", Development Initiatives, Paris, http://devinit.org/?dialogFeatures=protocol=http#!/post/the-role-of-the-private-sector-in-development-effectiveness-common-components-for-success-in-future-partnerships.

Di Bella, J. et al. (2013), "Mapping private sector engagements in development cooperation, The North-South Institute, Ottawa, www.nsi-ins.ca/publications/mapping-private-sector-engagements-in-development-cooperation.

Garside, B. et al. (2016), "Aid and business for sustainable development – Emerging lessons from effective aid-business partnerships in the era of the SDGs", Institute for Environment and Development, London, http://pubs.iied.org/16607IIED.html.

GIZ (2016), "lab of tomorrow" (PowerPoint slides), www.giz.de/Wirtschaft/de/downloads/giz2016-en-information-faq.pdf.

Government of the Netherlands (n.d.), "Public-private partnerships", www.government.nl/topics/development-cooperation/contents/development-cooperation-partners-and-partnerships/public-private-partnerships (accessed 1 July 2016).

Guarnaschelli, S. et al. (2014), "Innovative financing for development: Scalable business models that produce economic, social, and environmental outcomes", Global Development Incubator, New York, Washington, DC, and Hong Kong, www.citifoundation.com/citi/foundation/pdf/innovative_financing_for_development.pdf.

Heinrich, M. (2015), "Private sector partnerships to promote economic development – An overview of donor funds and facilities", The Donor Committee for Enterprise Development, Cambridge, www.enterprise-development.org/wp-content/uploads/DCED_PPP_SynthesisNote_20Feb2015updatedNov2015.pdf.

International Dialogue on Peacebuilding and Statebuilding and BNP Paribas Investment Partners (forthcoming), "Investing in stability: Promoting more and better investment in post-conflict fragile and conflict-affected situations", OECD, Paris.

Kindornay, S., K. Higgins and M. Olender (2013), "Models for trade-related private sector partnerships for development", The North-South Institute, Ottawa, www.nsi-ins.ca/publications/models-for-trade-related-private-sector-partnerships-for-development.

Kindornay, S. and F. Reilly-King (2013), "Investing in the business of development: Bilateral donor approaches to engaging the private sector", The North-South Institute and Canadian Council for International Co-operation, Ottawa, www.nsi-ins.ca/publications/investing-in-the-business-of-development.

Kindornay, S., S. Tissot and N. Sheiban (2014), "The value of cross-sector development partnerships", The North-South Institute, Ottawa, www.nsi-ins.ca/wp-content/uploads/2014/01/The-Value-of-Cross-Sector-Development-Partnerships.pdf.

Kwakkenbos, J. (2012). "Private profit for public good? Can investing in private companies deliver for the poor?" European Network on Debt and Development, Brussels, http://eurodad.org/files/pdf/1543000-private-profit-for-public-good-can-investing-in-private-companies-deliver-for-the-poor-.pdf.

McKinsey & Company (2009), "Public-private partnerships: Harnessing the private sector's unique ability to enhance social impact", McKinsey & Company, Sydney, http://mckinseyonsociety.com/downloads/reports/Global-Public-Health/Public_Private_Partnerships_Enhancing_Social_Impact.pdf.

Ministry of Foreign Affairs of the Netherlands (2010), "A guide to public-private partnerships (PPPs): A practical handbook on launching an effective public-private partnership", Ministry of Foreign Affairs of the Netherlands, The Hague, www.minbuza.nl/binaries/content/assets/minbuza/en/import/en/key_topics/development_cooperation/partners_in_development/public_private_partnerships/a-guide-to-public-private-partnerships.

Missika, B. and E. Romon (2014), "Foundations as development partners", *Development Co-operation Report 2014: Mobilising Resources for Sustainable Development*, OECD Publishing, Paris, http://dx.doi.org/10.1787/dcr-2014-en.

Partnerships Resource Centre (2013), "How to make cross-sector partnerships work? Critical success factors for partnering", Partnerships Resource Centre, Rotterdam, www.rsm.nl/fileadmin/Images_NEW/Faculty_Research/Partnership_Resource_Centre/brochure-How-to-make-cross-partnerships-work-2013.pdf.

Pattberg, P. and O. Widerberg (2014), "Transnational multi-stakeholder partnerships for sustainable development: Building blocks for success", IVM Institute for Environmental Studies, Amsterdam, http://fragmentation.eu/wp-content/uploads/2014/08/R14-31-ICSC-report-FINAL.pdf.

Pfisterer, S. (2013), "Development partnerships with the private sector at work: Insights from partnerships with the private sector facilitated by the Dutch Embassy in Colombia", Partnerships Resource Centre, Rotterdam.

PPPlab (2014a), "Building partnerships", *Insights Series 02*, PPPLab Food & Water, Rotterdam, www.ppplab.org/wordpress/wp-content/uploads/2014/10/PPP-Serie-A2-spreads1.pdf.

PPPlab (2014b), "Public-private partnerships: A brief introduction", *Insights Series 01*, PPPLab Food & Water, Rotterdam, www.ppplab.org/wordpress/wp-content/uploads/2014/10/PPP-Serie-A1-spreads1.pdf.

Romero, M. (2014), "A private affair: Shining a light on the shadowy institutions giving public support to private companies and taking over the development agenda", European Network on Debt and Development, Brussels, www.eurodad.org/files/pdf/1546237-a-private-affair-shining-a-light-on-the-shadowy-institutions-giving-public-support-to-private-companies-and-taking-over-the-development-agenda.pdf (accessed 8 June 2016).

World Economic Forum and OECD (2015), "Blended finance vol. 1: A primer for development finance and philanthropic funders", World Economic Forum, Geneva, www3.weforum.org/docs/WEF_Blended_Finance_A_Primer_Development_Finance_Philanthropic_Funders_report_2015.pdf.

Private Sector Engagement for Sustainable Development:
Lessons from the DAC

Chapter 6

From risk to results in working with and through the private sector in development co-operation

This chapter examines risk management, leverage, additionality and issues related to measuring private sector engagements – results as well as monitoring and evaluation. Government institutions must be willing to take risks if they want to encourage the private sector to do likewise. Risk management strategies used by DAC members include the use of clear partnership criteria, drawing on expertise and evidence-based analysis to inform decision making, due diligence processes and careful attention to private sector motivations. The chapter provides an extensive analysis on the question of additionality in private sector engagements. It highlights that the concept of additionality is understood in a number of ways by different stakeholders and suggests the need for DAC members to establish systematic approaches to additionality assessment, commensurate with the size of investments. The discussion on results points to the significant gap in results reporting among DAC members at project, mechanism and portfolio levels, and calls for the use of standardised results indicators to measure outcomes and allow for comparability across private sector engagements. Finally, good practice suggests the need for government institutions to prioritise monitoring and evaluation of private sector engagements and invest in the creation of knowledge systems that promote learning and facilitate course correction.

Risk

An important rationale behind private sector engagements is that government can spur innovation and investment by redistributing some financial risk from the private sector to itself. This assumption is built into DAC members' financing modalities. With grant-based financing to the private sector, private sector partners are almost always required to match grant funds with their own resources. Non-concessional financing tools such as guarantees and political risk insurance also seek to promote private sector investment by reducing financial risk. In addition to financial risks, DAC members and their partners face reputational risks when partnering. For DAC members, it is important that private sector partners are good corporate citizens in a broad sense (Kindornay, Higgins and Olender, 2013).

Encouraging private sector risk taking

Government institutions must be willing to take risks if they want to encourage the private sector to do likewise. The peer learning review showed that government can promote greater risk taking on the part of the private sector by taking on relatively high risk. Large impacts often come with greater risks. In this context, good practice suggests the need to take a portfolio approach to private sector engagement which recognises that some investments will fail. Indeed, if all partnerships were successful, this would indicate that government is not being risky enough in supporting innovation through its engagements with the private sector.

A practical way to promote greater risk taking is for DAC members to serve as first movers on high-risk opportunities. For example, the country review of the Netherlands demonstrated the importance of being willing to take the first loss as an effective means to crowd in investments. The Netherlands was one of the first DAC members to provide support to the Currency Exchange Fund,[1] which, as noted in Chapter 4, now has 24 investors. In addition, by providing hedging products where previously no markets exist, the Currency Exchange Fund has operated as a market maker, encouraging other participants to enter markets.

> *Manage risk through clear partnership criteria, expertise and evidence-based analysis, due diligence and careful attention to private sector motivations.*

Risk-mitigation strategies

In their efforts to share risk with the private sector, it is critical that DAC members have effective risk-management strategies. Country reviews revealed a number of ways to effectively manage risk through clear partnership criteria, expertise and evidence-based analysis, due diligence and careful attention to private sector motivations.

The use of clear criteria for partnership is an effective mechanism for risk management. Transparent screening processes that include elements of responsible business conduct as a criterion for partnership can help DAC members attract and select partners that are good corporate citizens, which work to manage financial and reputational risks. Screening criteria can also provide a clear indication of exclusions, including the industries and types of partners with which DAC members are unwilling to work. This approach is also helpful for managing reputational risks that may be associated with different partners.

Developing in-house expertise and carrying out evidence-based analysis to inform partnerships are also critical tools for risk management. Willingness to invest in research and feasibility studies to ground interventions in a good understanding of the market and where opportunities exist is also a success factor. In the context of the Netherlands, this approach appears to be well established and appreciated by government and non-government stakeholders. In Germany, systems thinking is an important tool for ensuring the successful design of projects with the private sector and risk management. Systems thinking recognises the complexity in which development projects and partnerships operate. It includes outlining assumptions, logic and factors that can influence success inside and outside of a particular project. This approach can be used to outline risk associated with potential projects and partnerships.

Due diligence is necessary in private sector engagements, but should be commensurate with the size of investments. Government institutions are supporting a wide range of initiatives with the private sector, ranging from small investments with SMEs to large-scale multi-stakeholder partnerships and investments worth significant amounts of money. In both instances, DAC members have a responsibility to carry out due diligence on partners. However, due diligence processes should be streamlined according to the size of investments with more stringent processes applied to larger investments for which risks are greater.

Reviewed countries also noted that due diligence processes are insufficient to assess potential partners. Risk management and mitigation of adverse impacts are essential, but still only a step toward positive development contributions. A company may be able to pass due diligence processes and still not be a good partner. It is important to assess company interests and ensure that values are shared, as well as understand the people behind the company and their motivations.

Ensuring support for government risk taking

Low tolerance for risk by stakeholders, such as politicians and the general public, can present a challenge for private sector engagement. The United States has found that frequent communication of successes is an important way to tackle this challenge. It ensures that conversations with key stakeholders highlight successes often more frequently than failures, making it easier to discuss failures in the context of overall portfolios. The United States' experience also shows that it is important to educate stakeholders that working with the private sector carries intrinsic risks and that failures are not a sign that something is wrong, but that institutions are supporting innovation, and are adapting and evolving.

Leverage

Realistic expectations

Although private sector engagement is critical for realising sustainable development outcomes, there is a need to be realistic in terms of expectations for the private sector, particularly in terms of financing. The financing needed to realise the Sustainable Development Goals is great. The Sustainable Development Solutions Network estimates that the incremental financing needed to realise the Sustainable Development Goals in low- and middle-income countries will be USD 1.4 trillion per year, requiring a mix of government and private finance (Schmidt-Traub, 2015; see also Guarnaschelli et al., 2014). Schmidt-Traub (2015) estimates that about half of Sustainable Development Goal investments can be privately financed and that even with domestic resource mobilisation, there will be an external financing gap of USD 152-163 billion per year to be met by government finance, including ODA. In this context, DAC members are keen to leverage private finance through their contributions.

However, government financing that leverages the private sector still remains a relatively small part of overall development co-operation. In their examination of innovative financing, Guarnaschelli et al. (2014: vii) estimate that USD 11 billion in innovative financing resources were mobilised in 2012 (additional to aid) compared to USD 137 billion in official aid flows. The 2015 DAC survey on mobilisation of private sector finance by official development finance interventions, namely guarantees, syndicated loans and shares in collective investment vehicles, showed that over 2012-14, USD 36.4 billion was raised, with an upward trend occurring in more recent years (Benn et al., 2016). Mobilisation of private sector resources is growing yet overall figures suggest that discussions on the potential to leverage private investments through government finance need to set realistic expectations.

Ensuring leverage

As mentioned, DAC members make use of leverage ratios in their private sector engagements. Private sector partners must be willing to invest their own resources (finance or in-kind contributions) to benefit from government finance. This is an element of good practice identified through the peer learning review. Leverage ratios ensure all partners are fully committed to initiatives. At the same time, it should be recognised that although it is important to ensure all partners are fully committed, leverage ratios can have perverse incentives, particularly in terms of incentivising investments toward countries and sectors for which it is easier to raise private capital, rather than toward underserved markets where needs may be greatest though opportunities for leveraging are more limited. The higher the leverage ratio, the more the resources mobilised in proportion to the resources allocated by the government institution. However, the leverage ratio does not depend only on the mobilisation effect of a given financial instrument, but also on the context and market conditions in which the instrument is being used. It is likely that any instrument, if used in low-income countries, will have a lower leverage ratio than the same instrument used in a middle-income country (government efforts needed to make investments in low-income countries attractive to the private sector are likely to be more than the efforts needed in middle-income countries). It is important that DAC members ensure commitments by all partners to initiatives while ensuring that efforts to leverage private finance do not create perverse allocation incentives.

Communicating leverage

Reporting on leverage can be an important way to garner political support for private sector engagements in development co-operation. USAID reports on the amount of private finance it leverages on an annual basis as part of its commitment to better engage the private sector in development co-operation.[2]

Though leverage is often understood in financial terms, some DAC members note that it is important to understand leverage in terms of tangible and intangible impacts. For Sweden, leveraging the private sector is not about financing alone. The process of engagement changes mindsets in the private sector and approaches to conducting core business. Engagement has potential for long-term effects beyond any individual partnership, including the finance leveraged from the private sector.

Additionality

Understanding additionality

Discussions during the workshop on additionality in Luxembourg highlighted that the concept of additionality is understood in various ways by different stakeholders (Box 6.1). Assessments of private sector engagements in development co-operation have pointed to financial and development additionality (Kindornay and Reilly-King, 2013; Pereira, 2015, see also Heinrich, 2013). At the workshop, representatives from DFIs also highlighted value additionality.

Box 6.1. **Understanding additionality**

"In the context of reporting on private sector instruments in DAC statistics, [the OECD-DAC Secretariat has proposed that] an official transaction is considered additional either because of its 'financial additionality' or 'value additionality' or both.

Such a transaction is financially additional if it is extended to an entity which cannot obtain finance from the private capital markets (local or international) with similar terms or quantities without official support, or if it mobilises investment from the private sector that would not have otherwise invested.

It is additional in value if the official sector offers to recipient entities or mobilises, alongside its investment, non-financial value that the private sector is not offering and which will lead to better development outcomes, e.g. by providing or catalysing knowledge and expertise, promoting social or environmental standards or fostering good corporate governance" (DCD-DAC-STAT, 2016: 7).

In addition to financial and value additionality, literature on additionality also often refers to development additionality. This form of additionality refers to the development impacts that arise as a result of the investment that otherwise would not have occurred. In this case, one of the main rationales for partnership is that it facilitates faster, larger or better development impacts than the private sector or government would be able to achieve working alone.

Different forms of additionality are not mutually exclusive and are necessarily linked. For example, the knowledge and expertise of government institutions (value additionality) generally contribute to ensuring better quality investments from a development perspective and, in turn, greater development impacts (development additionality). During the workshop, participants noted that it is helpful to frame additionality in these different ways. They also agreed on the importance of overarching principles such as do no harm and avoiding market distortion as critical to additionality. Generally speaking, there is more consensus on the meaning of financial additionality than there is on value additionality, while the concept of development additionality may be a newer one for some DAC members.

Ensuring additionality

Additionality is a factor whenever the private sector is engaged in development co-operation through the use of government funds. The question of whether government is supporting the private sector to do something it otherwise would not have done without government support is always relevant and should inform the decision to engage with potential partners. In this sense, additionality matters for most private sector engagement modalities including private sector instruments,[3] advisory services and technical assistance.

Despite the widespread recognition of the importance of ensuring additionality in private sector engagements, DAC members and others continue to face criticism over the lack of transparency on how they assess additionality (Kindornay and Reilly-King, 2013; Pereira, 2015). Moreover, research has shown that there is a lack of internal guidelines and systems across government institutions that engage the private sector in development co-operation to assess additionality (Heinrich, 2013). For some institutions, assessment criteria are limited or vague. In some cases, institutions rely exclusively on companies to say why support is needed and it is unclear how this information is rigorously assessed. Others institutions have no internal guidelines on how additionality is assessed, documented and communicated externally. The lack of internal guidelines undermines transparency and limits the ability of staff to consistently assess additionality.

There is a need for transparent narratives on additionality for projects that are linked to expected development impacts.

The lack of guidelines also likely contributes to limited communication on additionality for projects with the private sector. Given the importance that DAC members place on additionality, there is a need for transparent narratives on additionality for projects that are linked to expected development impacts. Institutions are often asked to showcase partnerships with the private sector. Without a compelling narrative as to why support is being provided, institutions open themselves up to criticism in the media and by other stakeholders that may misinterpret how institutions are working with the private sector and the rationale for doing so.

There is a need for DAC members to establish systems to ensure and measure additionality. A systematic approach to additionality assessment contributes to ensuring that private sector partnerships do not harm or distort markets, effectively harness the comparative advantages of government institutions and realise better development results. Moreover, such assessments can be used to set out a compelling case for government support to private sector partnerships. Yet, how additionality is ensured depends on the government institution involved. There is no harmonised practice across DFIs or among aid agencies to assess and ensure additionality when working with the private sector. Given that mandates, modes of operation and strategic objectives vary, government institutions address the question of additionality differently in practice (Box 6.2).

Box 6.2. **Methods for ensuring additionality**

Some institutions have developed systematic assessment frameworks and guidelines to assess financial, development and value additionality for individual projects. DFIs have played a leading role in this area. The German Investment and Development Corporation (DEG), Germany's DFI, has developed the Corporate-Policy Project Rating tool. The tool assesses financial and value additionality and expected development outcomes, is integrated into investment decision-making processes and is used throughout the life of an investment to monitor development outcomes. CDC Group plc, the United Kingdom's DFI, has developed a set of guidelines that are used for all investments to ensure financial and value additionality. In 2016, it introduced a process for ex post evaluations to assess value additionality.

For its part, the Donor Committee for Enterprise Development developed a framework to assess additionality ex ante based on eight criteria (Heinrich, 2014). These are grouped into three sub-categories: 1) resources, capabilities and incentives of the applicant; 2) resources that are available from other parties; and 3) engagement beyond the cost-shared project or partner business (value additionality). The framework offers a set of questions that institutions should ask to ensure additionality when working with the private sector.

In addition to assessments of individual projects, others make use of portfolio assessments. For example, Norfund, Norway's DFI, works only in the countries or sectors where markets are well known to be constrained and where risks are considered sufficiently high that commercial investors are unlikely to invest. A recent review of Norfund noted that the institution's portfolio approach to additionality that concentrates investments in high-risk countries and regions, combined with assessments of individual projects, works to ensure that its investments are additional (Gaia Consulting Ltd., 2015). The value of combining portfolio and individual project assessments of additionality was noted by participants at the additionality workshop.

Notwithstanding differences between government institutions, some elements that could be included in additionality guidelines were highlighted through the peer learning review. DAC members' guidelines should include stipulations to ensure additionality at the start of an investment and measure additionality ex post. Assessments of financial additionality should be made ex ante based on what is relevant at the time of the commitment. It is more difficult to assess financial additionality ex post. Markets change over time and what is additional today may not be additional in two years' time or vice versa. However, institutions can only work with and account for the information they have at the time when decisions are made. Though some attempts have been made to assess financial additionality ex post, this approach tends to be challenging partly because once a contract has ended, private sector partners are under no obligation to respond to requests for information, plus information provided by private sector partners may not be reliable. A key challenge for independent external evaluations of financial additionality is that there is no way to truly know if government support was additional without knowing full details about companies and projects, information which may be confidential.

Value and development additionality lend themselves to ex ante and ex post assessment. For value additionality, institutions can articulate their comparative advantages in partnerships, including what they plan to offer over the course of partnership. From the initial assessment of value additionality, partners can easily be asked to assess the extent to which they benefited from partnership with the government institution in terms of value additionality ex post. This type of assessment can facilitate structured feedback to institutions on their role in partnerships and inform their role in the future.

In terms of development additionality, expected development results should be articulated ex ante, including with reference to how results will be achieved more quickly, with greater impact or on a larger scale as a result of partnership. Assessment of development results should then be part of regular monitoring and evaluation reviews.

Also, it is useful for DAC members to monitor the assumptions that led to the conclusion that government resources were needed and are leading to impacts. Ex ante and ex post evaluations are important. However, it is equally important to define and monitor the assumptions that inform investment decisions. Monitoring assumptions offers opportunities for course correction over project life cycles, as well as to assess and learn from assumptions when partnering with the private sector over time.

In the creation of systems to ensure additionality, DAC members should be realistic about the costs and capacity constraints associated with generating evidence and preparing additionality assessments. Assessing additionality requires staff time and technical expertise. At the same time, institutions face pressure to reduce their overhead costs. Institutions also typically rely on information that is provided by private sector applicants. Though triangulation of this information is ideal, institutions are also constrained in terms of what information can be shared with others by in-house capacities and the costs associated with bringing in independent evaluators.

Approaches to additionality should take into consideration the costs of preparing assessments in proportion to the size of investments.

While government institutions carry out due diligence efforts by assessing market conditions, potential partners and proposals, providing hard evidence is difficult. Information provided with proposals is typically confidential and institutions face information asymmetries – they cannot know what other finance providers would be willing to do. There is no one-size-fits-all approach to additionality, as mentioned, and it is difficult to prove what would have happened otherwise. Given these challenges, approaches to additionality should take into consideration the costs of preparing assessments in proportion to the size of investments.

At a practical level, approaches to additionality, including the rigour at which it is ensured, may need to be adjusted according to investment type. For smaller investments, a rigorous assessment of additionality may not be feasible or desirable. Rather, applicants may be required to articulate why government support is needed, from which a decision is made. For larger investments, more rigorous assessments are likely to be required.

The type of partner also matters. For example, when working with smaller companies or start-ups, financial additionality must also carefully consider the sustainability of the investment, whereas with larger companies, financial sustainability is less likely to be an issue. Moreover, in some cases, different forms of additionality may play a greater role in prompting engagement. For example, when working with larger companies, value additionality and likelihood of significant development impacts may serve as the primary rationales for partnership. In the preparation of guidelines and systems to ensure additionality, DAC members should consider how their approach will vary depending on the size of investments and the different objectives that may inform private sector engagements.

Institutions may not be fully additional 100% of the time in the financial sense and still realise significant development impacts.

Additionality in practice

In practice, government institutions may not be fully additional 100% of the time in the financial sense and still realise significant development impacts. Ensuring financial additionality is not a perfect science. While ideally every deal should be additional, it is highly unlikely that institutions can guarantee that all deals are 100% additional all the time at the portfolio level. What is important to keep in consideration is development impacts, the total increase in investments that occurs in response to support provided by institutions (even if some investments in the portfolio may have gone ahead without government support) and the role of institutions in creating more and better business over time.

Finally, an important consideration with respect to financial additionality is its relationship to leverage. Political pressure for high leverage may reduce additionality. There is a danger of having too strong of a focus on leverage ratios in institutions. The focus on mobilising private capital may incentivise fund managers to be risk-averse and choose well-capitalised partners. Deals that raise higher amounts of capital tend to be less additional, while those that mobilise less capital tend to be more additional owing to the higher levels of risk associated with them. It is important to balance concern about leveraging additional funds with equal concern for ensuring financial additionality (avoiding market distortions) in partnerships and realising development results.

Results

Measuring results

A key criticism of private sector engagements in development is the limited demonstration of concrete results. A recent best practice guide on private sector partnerships reads: "After more than a decade of development partnerships, hard data on these partnerships' 'return on investment' for the public sector in terms of development achievements remains scarce and unsystematic" (Tewes-Gradl et al., 2014: 12). As DAC members expand and consolidate their private sector engagement portfolios, there is a significant need to better demonstrate and communicate results at project, programme and portfolio levels.

An important challenge that was noted in every country review is the adaptation of existing data management and information systems to effectively track private sector engagements and report on results. For many DAC members, the effective tracking of private sector engagement activities may require new and updated data management and information systems. For example, institutions participate in non-financial forms of private sector engagement, such as policy dialogue, that do not necessarily trigger a financial flow, but may lead to development results through the adoption of new standards. These types of activities may not be captured by regular data management and information systems.[4] Funding for private sector engagement that is channelled through a non-profit implementing partner also may not be captured by existing systems as part of private sector engagements. Without a specific marker, it is not evident which projects and activities include private sector partners. Notwithstanding ongoing efforts to include private sector instruments in the Creditor Reporting System, conversations with DAC members over the course of the peer learning review suggest that it may be useful for the OECD to develop a specific marker for private sector engagements that could capture flows related to policy dialogue and support for implementing partners, for example.

In terms of individual partnerships, there is a need to adapt results frameworks to meet the needs of all partners. Companies often have specific results that they work to achieve through partnership and their own rigorous evaluation systems and capacities to carry out evaluations. The same is true for government and civil society partners. It is important to develop appropriate results metrics that meet the needs of all partners. Tewes-Gradl et al. (2014) suggest that an effective approach is for partners to co-create results indicators and agree on how monitoring and evaluation will occur from the outset of partnership.

There is a need for standard results indicators to facilitate results comparison across projects, portfolios and implementing partners, as well as contribute to developing an overall results narrative.

Though it is important for DAC members to have some flexibility in determining results metrics with partners, the review also pointed to a need for standard results indicators to facilitate results comparison across projects, portfolios and implementing partners, as well as contribute to developing an overall results narrative. DAC members should look to central policy objectives for this purpose and make use of existing results metrics. It can be useful to have core outcome indicators for all sectors as well as specific indicators for each sector. OPIC makes use of this model in its approach to results measurement.

Results metrics can draw on existing frameworks. For instance, Impact Reporting and Investment Standards provides a list of commonly used indicators to assess company performance against financial, environmental and social outcomes.[5] Similarly, development indicators can be harmonised with other reporting standards, such as the Global Reporting Initiative,[6] as a way to reduce the reporting burden on companies (Tewes-Gradl et al., 2014). DFIs have also developed a set of Harmonized Indicators for Private Sector Operations.[7] DFIs have prepared 38 quantitative indicators, including cross-cutting indicators, for use across 15 sectors and industries. Fifteen of the indicators are aligned with the Impact Reporting and Investment Standards metrics. As a next step in this process, DFIs are looking to develop shared qualitative indicators. There is a variety of approaches and options available for the standardisation of results indicators in relation to private sector engagement. Once established, such indicators can be used to set out overall results narratives, which have the potential to garner further support for private sector engagement activities and ensure greater accountability.

The establishment of provisions for results monitoring up front in individual private sector engagements is a recognised element of best practice (Tewes-Gradl et al., 2014). DAC members' experiences show that establishing clear provisions for monitoring at the initial planning phase of partnerships is important for ensuring that all partners have a common understanding of what is expected and that resources are allocated appropriately. A balance is needed between reporting on activities and results during project life cycles and ensuring that reporting is not too burdensome, particularly for relatively smaller investments or when working with relatively smaller companies. In this sense, provisions and resources allocated for monitoring should be proportionate to the size of investments.

Communicating results

In line with other studies on private sector engagements in development co-operation, the peer learning review identified results reporting on individual projects and at the portfolio level as a major gap that urgently needs to be addressed to improve transparency and demonstrate the value of private sector engagement. There are examples of good practice, however. DEG and OPIC provide results on individual investments as well as at the portfolio level. In its 2014 report on development co-operation results, the Netherlands included a review of private sector development, which includes its private sector engagement activities. The report makes use of international indicators related to private sector development, such as the World Bank's ease of doing business index, and aggregates the results from the Netherlands' private sector engagement activities to provide data and information on six thematic areas: *1)* market access and sustainable trade; *2)* laws, regulations and policy plans; *3)* economic institutions and actors; *4)* infrastructure development; *5)* financial sector development; and *6)* private investment in developing countries (Ministry of Foreign Affairs of the Netherlands, 2015c).

It can be challenging enough to communicate on the tangible results of the private sector. Indeed, existing results systems do not fully capture the range of impacts and benefits of working with the private sector. This is particularly true in the case of policy dialogue and co-creation processes, which may lead to significant changes in business models and approaches, but may not include financial disbursements. It can be beneficial for DAC members to report on the results of engagements that do not always lead to concrete projects. Such reporting can help to explain the value of policy dialogue and other modalities for private sector engagement to internal and external stakeholders.

Evaluation

As with the case of results reporting, rigorous evaluations of private sector engagements have been insufficient. While DAC members evaluate their private sector engagements,[8] the peer learning review revealed that, in comparison to the scope of activities being undertaken with the private sector, there is likely a need for greater attention to and rigour of evaluations. Moreover, the review found that existing evaluations do not always sufficiently capture the development impacts of private sector engagements. Evaluations of the United States' Global Development Alliances, for example, tend to be more descriptive than analytic. In a meta-review of evaluations of the Netherlands' private sector engagement mechanisms, the independent Policy and Operations Evaluation Department of the Ministry of Foreign Affairs of the Netherlands found that evaluations neither sufficiently examine the effectiveness of PPPs resulting from private sector mechanisms nor sufficiently focus on the ultimate objectives of PPPs, namely improving incomes, reducing poverty and realising economic growth (Bouman et al., 2013). As a result of this work, the Policy and Operations Evaluation Department recommended that mechanisms and future evaluations conduct baseline studies, systematically collect quantitative data at the impact level, and carry out evaluations at the programme level. It also suggested that evaluations should not be limited to individual projects, but should rather focus on studying the added value of the mechanism as a whole.

Resourcing an effective approach to evaluation

The peer learning review revealed that there is a need for greater investment in evaluations of private sector engagements at individual project, sector and portfolio levels. There is a gap in terms of ex ante and ex post additionality assessments, as well as portfolio-wide reviews of private sector partnerships (though some good examples emerged from the peer learning review). The application of appropriate independent evaluation processes is important for assessing development impacts, communicating results and driving evidence-based decision making. Notably, DEG makes use of thematic and portfolio evaluations. In DEG's experience, thematic evaluations are useful for identifying best practice and learning both within and across institutions. Portfolio evaluations offer opportunities to assess impacts and inform future investments. The peer learning review also showed that the use of external bodies, including knowledge partners, to assess and feed into evaluation processes can enhance their credibility inside and outside government. As noted in Chapter 5, the Netherlands works with research institutions to evaluate partnerships and their impacts.

As with the case of monitoring results, provisions for evaluation should be established at the initial stages of partnership. This approach is important to ensure that evaluation is a central feature of project design and not an afterthought.

Ensure that new approaches and initiatives build on lessons from evaluations.

Learning from evaluation

Evaluations of private sector engagements alone are not enough. Efforts are needed to ensure that new approaches and initiatives build on lessons from evaluations. Effective knowledge management systems are needed to ensure lessons and best practice feed into strategic planning processes and subsequent activities. US government institutions that engage the private sector collect data and conduct research to better understand the results and lessons from private sector engagement activities as well as inform future approaches and strategies for engaging the private sector. For example, a number of reports have been produced by looking at the effectiveness of Global Development Alliances by USAID and external evaluators (see US Peer Learning Report).[9]

Overall, evaluation culture is something that must be actively established and fostered. The Netherlands' experience shows that legal and regulatory requirements – evaluation protocols – can lead to increased attention to and appreciation of monitoring and evaluation. Management within government institutions must make evaluation and learning priorities that are supported by internal policies and systems as well as human and financial resources.

Notes

1. As noted in Chapter 4, the fund provides products to hedge the currency and interest rate mismatches that are created when international investors lend to financial institutions in partner countries in their local currencies. For more information on the Currency Exchange Fund, see: www.oecd.org/dac/peer-reviews/Currency-Exchange-Fund.pdf.
2. See www.usaid.gov/usaidforward. It should be noted that it is often more difficult to measure leverage for more complex mechanisms that go beyond one-to-one matching. See Griffiths for a discussion (2012).
3. Additionality will be a key criterion for assessing the ODA eligibility of private sector instruments and therefore it will be monitored in the DAC statistical system.
4. In some instances, effort is measurable in terms of staff resources, salaries or other costs for the DAC member. In these cases, it is reportable and trackable in the Creditor Reporting System.
5. See https://iris.thegiin.org.
6. See www.globalreporting.org/Pages/default.aspx.
7. See https://indicators.ifipartnership.org.
8. For more information, see: www.oecd.org/dac/peer-reviews/DAC-Member-Evaluations-of-Private-Sector-Engagements.pdf.
9. For more information, see: www.oecd.org/dac/peer-reviews/Peer-Learning-Country-Report-United-States.pdf.

References

ADB (n.d.), "Social development and poverty: Inclusive business", https://www.adb.org/themes/social-development/inclusive-business (accessed 4 July 2016).

Benn, J. et al. (2016), "Amounts mobilised from the private sector by official development finance interventions: Guarantees, syndicated loans and shares in collective investment vehicles", *OECD Development Co-operation Working Papers*, No. 26, OECD Publishing, Paris, http://dx.doi.org/10.1787/5jm3xh459n37-en.

BoP Global Network (2012), "BoP concept", www.bopglobalnetwork.org/bop-concept (accessed 28 July 2016).

BoP Innovation Center (n.d.), "Base of the pyramid", http://bopinnovationcenter.com/what-we-do/base-of-the-pyramid (accessed 28 July 2016).

Bouman, S. et al. (2013), "Public-private partnerships in developing countries: A systematic literature review", *IOB Study*, No. 378, Ministry of Foreign Affairs of the Netherlands, The Hague, www.government.nl/documents/reports/2013/06/13/iob-study-public-private-partnerships-in-developing-countries.

Commonwealth of Australia (2015), "Creating shared value through partnership: Ministerial statement on engaging the private sector in aid and development", Department of Foreign Affairs and Trade, Canberra, http://dfat.gov.au/about-us/publications/aid/Pages/creating-shared-value-through-partnership.aspx.

Crishna Morgado, N. et al. (forthcoming), "Development co-operation and private sector engagement for the environment – a scoping paper", OECD Publishing, Paris.

DEG (2013), "Corporate-policy project rating (GPR)", German Investment and Development Corporation, Cologne, www.deginvest.de/DEG-Englische-Dokumente/About-DEG/Our-Mandate/Detailed-GPR-Description.pdf.

Di Bella, J. et al. (2013), "Mapping private sector engagements in development cooperation, The North-South Institute, Ottawa, www.nsi-ins.ca/publications/mapping-private-sector-engagements-in-development-cooperation.

EPEC (n.d.), "Bankability", www.eib.org/epec/g2g/i-project-identification/12/123/index.htm (accessed 28 July 2016).

Gaia Consulting Ltd. (2015), "Evaluation of the Norwegian Investment Fund for Developing Countries (Norfund)", Norwegian Agency for Development Cooperation, Oslo, www.norfund.no/getfile.php/136301/Documents/Homepage/Reports%20and%20presentations/Evaluation%20of%20the%20Norwegian%20Investment%20Fund%20for%20Developing%20Countries.pdf.

GIIN (n.d.), "What you need to know about impact investing", https://thegiin.org/impact-investing/need-to-know/#s2 (accessed 4 July 2016).

Gradl, C. and C. Knobloch (2010), "Inclusive business guide: How to develop business and fight poverty", endeva, Berlin, www.endeva.org/wp-content/uploads/2014/11/IBG_final.pdf.

Griffiths, J. (2012), "'Leveraging' private sector finance: How does it work and what are the risks?", The Bretton Woods Project, Washington, www.brettonwoodsproject.org/wp-content/uploads/2013/10/leveraging.pdf (accessed 6 June 2016).

Guarnaschelli, S. et al. (2014), "Innovative financing for development: Scalable business models that produce economic, social, and environmental outcomes", Global Development Incubator, New York, Washington, DC, and Hong Kong, www.citifoundation.com/citi/foundation/pdf/innovative_financing_for_development.pdf.

Heinrich, M. (2014), "Demonstrating additionality in private sector development initiatives: A practical exploration of good practice for challenge funds and other cost-sharing mechanisms", The Donor Committee for Enterprise Development, Cambridge, www.enterprise-development.org/implementing-psd/private-sector-engagement-and-partnerships/demonstrating-additionality-dced-publication.

Heinrich, M. (2013), "Donor partnerships with business for private sector development: What can we learn from experience?", The Donor Committee for Enterprise Development, Cambridge, www.enterprise-development.org/wp-content/uploads/DCEDWorkingPaper_PartnershipsforPSDLearningFromExperience_26Mar2013.pdf.

Investopedia (2016), "Corporate social responsibility", www.investopedia.com/terms/c/corp-social-responsibility.asp (accessed 4 July 2016).

ISO (2014), "ISO 26000:2010; Guidance on social responsibility", www.iso.org/iso/catalogue_detail?csnumber=42546.

Kindornay, S., K. Higgins and M. Olender (2013), "Models for trade-related private sector partnerships for development", The North-South Institute, Ottawa, www.nsi-ins.ca/publications/models-for-trade-related-private-sector-partnerships-for-development.

Kindornay, S. and F. Reilly-King (2013), "Investing in the business of development: Bilateral donor approaches to engaging the private sector", The North-South Institute and Canadian Council for International Co-operation, Ottawa, www.nsi-ins.ca/publications/investing-in-the-business-of-development.

Ministry of Foreign Affairs of the Netherlands (2015), "Results private sector development 2014", Ministry of Foreign Affairs of the Netherlands, The Hague, www.rijksoverheid.nl/documenten/kamerstukken/2015/11/06/bijlage-28.

OECD (2016a), "DAC High Level Meeting communiqué", OECD Publishing, Paris, www.oecd.org/dac/DAC-HLM-Communique-2016.pdf.

OECD (2016b), "Implementation of the principles of ODA modernisation on private-sector instruments: Template for the ODA-eligibility assessment of DFIs and other vehicles and definitions and reporting on additionality", DCD/DAC/STAT(2016)1/Rev2, OECD, Paris, www.oecd.org/officialdocuments/publicdisplaydocumentpdf/?cote=DCD/DAC/STAT%282016%291&docLanguage=En.

OECD (2015a), "Inclusion of the effort in using private-sector instruments in ODA: Exploring further the institutional and instrument-specific approaches", DCD/DAC/STAT(2015)3, OECD, Paris, www.oecd.org/officialdocuments/publicdisplaydocumentpdf/?cote=DCD/DAC/STAT(2015)3&docLanguage=En (accessed 2 June 2016).

OECD (2015b), *Policy Framework for Investment 2015 Edition*, OECD Publishing, Paris, http://dx.doi.org/10.1787/9789264208667-en.

OECD (2014a), "OECD Guidelines for Multinational Enterprises: Responsible business conduct matters", OECD Publishing, Paris, https://mneguidelines.oecd.org/MNEguidelines_RBCmatters.pdf.

OECD (2014b), "Using financial instruments to mobilise private investment for development", in OECD, *Development Co-operation Report 2014: Mobilising Resources for Sustainable Development*, OECD Publishing, Paris, http://dx.doi.org/10.1787/dcr-2014-15-en.

Pereira, J. (2015), "Leveraging aid: A literature review on the additionality of using ODA to leverage private investments", UK Aid Network, London, www.ukan.org.uk/wordpress/wp-content/uploads/2015/03/UKAN-Leveraging-Aid-Literature-Review-03.15.pdf (accessed 8 June 2016).

Sandor, E., S. Scott and J. Benn (2009), "Innovative financing to fund development: Progress and prospects", *DCD Issues Brief*, OECD Publishing, Paris, www.oecd.org/development/effectiveness/44087344.pdf.

Schmidt-Traub, G. (2015), "Investment needs to achieve the sustainable development goals: Understanding the billions and trillions", *SDSN Working Paper*, Version 2, Sustainable Development Solutions Network, New York, http://unsdsn.org/wp-content/uploads/2015/09/151112-SDG-Financing-Needs.pdf.

Tewes-Gradl, C. et al. (2014), "Proving and improving the impact of development partnerships: 12 good practices for results measurement", Endeva UG, Berlin, www.endeva.org/publication/proving-and-improving-the-impact-of-development-partnerships.

UN (2011), "Guiding Principles on Business and Human Rights: Implementing the United Nations 'Protect, Respect and Remedy' Framework", United Nations, New York and Geneva, www.ohchr.org/Documents/Publications/GuidingPrinciplesBusinessHR_EN.pdf.

World Economic Forum and OECD (2015), "Blended finance vol. 1: A primer for development finance and philanthropic funders", World Economic Forum, Geneva, www3.weforum.org/docs/WEF_Blended_Finance_A_Primer_Development_Finance_Philanthropic_Funders_report_2015.pdf.

Private Sector Engagement for Sustainable Development:
Lessons from the DAC

ANNEX A

Overview of DAC member policy frameworks on private sector engagement

Country	Policy framework and focus
Australia	Commonwealth of Australia (2015a), "Creating shared value through partnership: Ministerial statement on engaging the private sector in aid and development", Department of Foreign Affairs and Trade, Canberra, http://dfat.gov.au/about-us/publications/aid/Pages/creating-shared-value-through-partnership.aspx. • Ministerial statement on engaging the private sector in aid and development: Focuses on private sector engagement.
	Commonwealth of Australia (2015b), "Strategy for Australia's aid investments in private sector development", Department of Foreign Affairs and Trade, Canberra, http://dfat.gov.au/about-us/publications/Documents/strategy-for-australias-investments-in-private-sector-development.pdf. • Creating shared value through partnership: Focuses on private sector development.
Austria	Austrian Development Agency (2013), "Three-year programme on Austrian development policy 2013-2015", Federal Ministry for European and International Affairs, Vienna, www.entwicklung.at/fileadmin/user_upload/Dokumente/Publikationen/3_JP/Englisch/2013-2015_3-YP.pdf. • Includes private sector and development as a priority, referring to both private sector development in partner countries and private sector engagement.
	Austrian Development Agency (2010), "Wirtschaft und Entwicklung: Leitlinien der Österreichischen Entwicklungszusammenarbeit [Economy and development: Guidelines of the Austrian Development Cooperation]", Austrian Development Agency, Vienna, www.entwicklung.at/fileadmin/user_upload/Dokumente/Publikationen/Downloads_Themen_DivBerichte/Wirtschaft/LL_WuE_April2010_03.pdf. • Strategy on private sector and development (German only): Includes three pillars, two of which are related to private sector development with a third that focuses on private sector engagement.
Belgium	Belgium (2014), "Note stratégique: Coopération belge au développement et secteur privé local : un appui au service du développement humain durable", Belgian Foreign Affairs, Foreign Trade and Development Cooperation, Brussels, http://diplomatie.belgium.be/sites/default/files/downloads/note_secteur_prive.pdf. • Local private sector development strategy (French only): Focuses largely on private sector development in partner countries, though outlines the role of Belgium's DFI, the Belgian Investment Company for Developing Countries (BIO), in supporting businesses under the strategy.
	No specific strategy on private sector engagement.
Canada	Canadian International Development Agency (2010), "Stimulating sustainable economic growth: CIDA's sustainable economic growth strategy", Canadian International Development Agency, Ottawa, www.acdi-cida.gc.ca/INET/IMAGES.NSF/vLUImages/EconomicGrowth/$file/Sustainable-Economic-Growth-e.pdf. • Includes provisions to support private sector development.
	Private sector as partners in development (website), www.international.gc.ca/development-developpement/partners-partenaires/ps-sp.aspx?lang=eng. • Overview of private sector engagement approaches.
Czech Republic	Ministry of Foreign Affairs of the Czech Republic (2010), "Development cooperation strategy of the Czech Republic 2010–2017", Ministry of Foreign Affairs of the Czech Republic, Prague, www.mzv.cz/file/762314/FINAL__Development_Cooperation_Strategy_2010_2017.pdf • Development Cooperation Strategy: Includes reference to private sector engagement through specific mechanisms.
	No specific strategy on private sector engagement.
Denmark	Ministry of Foreign Affairs of Denmark (2011), "Strategic framework for priority area: Growth and employment 2011-2015", Ministry of Foreign Affairs of Denmark, Copenhagen, http://um.dk/en/danida-en/goals/strategic-framework/growth-and-employment-strategy-2011-15. • Includes provisions on private sector development and private sector engagement.
European Union	European Commission (2014), "A Stronger Role of the Private Sector in Achieving Inclusive and Sustainable Growth in Developing Countries", European Commission, Brussels, http://eur-lex.europa.eu/legal-content/EN/TXT/PDF/?uri=CELEX%3A52014DC0263&qid=1400681732387&from=EN. • Communication: Includes provisions on private sector development and private sector engagement.
Finland	Ministry of Foreign Affairs of Finland (2012), "Creating jobs through private sector and trade development: Aid for trade – Finland's action plan 2012–2015", Ministry of Foreign Affairs of Finland, Helsinki, http://formin.finland.fi/public/default.aspx?contentid=263729&nodeid=49542&contentlan=2&culture=en-US. • Includes provisions on private sector development and private sector engagement
France	No publicly available policy framework, however information is available on the French Development Agency's website on private sector development and private sector engagement-related activities

Country	Policy framework and focus
Germany	BMZ (2013), "Sector strategy on private sector development", *BMZ Strategy Paper*, No. 9/2013e, Federal Ministry for Economic Cooperation and Development, Bonn and Berlin, www.bmz.de/en/publications/archiv/type_of_publication/strategies/Strategiepapier338_09_2013.pdf. • Focuses on private sector development and includes linkages with private sector engagement.
	BMZ (2011a), "Developing markets, creating wealth, reducing poverty, taking responsibility – The private sector as a partner of development policy", *BMZ Strategy Paper*, No. 304, Federal Ministry for Economic Cooperation and Development, Bonn and Berlin, www.bmz.de/en/publications/archiv/type_of_publication/strategies/Strategiepapier304_03_2011.pdf. • Focuses on private sector engagement with links to private sector development.
	Germany also has a range of other policies that inform its private sector engagement and private sector development activities. These include strategies for financial systems development, aid for trade, and the use of social and ecological market economy principles in development co-operation.
Greece	No publicly available policy framework.
Iceland	No publicly available policy framework.
Ireland	Department of Foreign Affairs and Trade (2013), "One world, one future – Ireland's policy for international development", Government of Ireland, Dublin, www.irishaid.ie/media/irishaid/allwebsitemedia/20newsandpublications/publicationpdfsenglish/one-world-one-future-irelands-new-policy.pdf. • Includes private sector development (through priority of trade and economic growth).
	Department of Foreign Affairs and Trade (2011), "Ireland and Africa: Our partnership with a changing continent", Government of Ireland, Dublin, www.irishaid.ie/media/irishaid/allwebsitemedia/20newsandpublications/publicationpdfsenglish/africa-strategy.pdf. • Includes reference to private sector development and private sector engagement (though does not spell out overall approach to private sector engagement).
	No specific strategy on private sector engagement.
Italy	Ministero degli Affari Esteri e della Coorperazione Internazionale [Ministry of Foreign Affairs and International Cooperation] (2014), "Italy's development cooperation in the 2014-2016 three-year period: Programme guidelines and orientations", Ministero degli Affari Esteri e della Coorperazione Internazionale [Ministry of Foreign Affairs and International Cooperation], Rome, www.cooperazioneallosviluppo.esteri.it/pdgcs/Documentazione/DocumentiNew/MAE_Guidelines%202014-2016_ENG.pdf. • Includes provisions on private sector development and private sector engagement.
	No specific strategy on private sector engagement.
Japan	Public-Private Partnership for Growth in Developing Countries (2008, unavailable) Includes provisions for private sector engagement with linkages to promoting private sector development
Korea	KOICA (2015), "Korea Mid-term ODA Policy for 2016-2020", Korea International Cooperation Agency, Seoul, www.odakorea.go.kr/ODAPage_2012/T02/L01_S04_02.jsp. (Korean only) • Includes reference to diversification of private partnership and promotion of inclusive business model KOICA (2011), "KOICA mid-term CSOs and private sector partnership strategy for 2011-2015", Korea International Cooperation Agency, Seoul. (Korean only) • Korea International Cooperation Agency strategy refers to private sector engagement EDCF Mid-term Strategic Plan to promote engagement of and partnership with the private sector in the global infrastructure development (Korean only, unavailable) • Korea Export-Import Bank strategy refers to private sector engagement
Luxembourg	Ministry of Foreign and European Affairs (2014), "Plan d'action pour l'efficacité du développement 2014-2016 [Action plan for development effectiveness 2014-2016]", Ministry of Foreign and European Affairs, Luxembourg, http://cooperation.mae.lu/fr/Actualites-Cooperation/Plan-d-action-pour-l-efficacite-du-developpement-2014-2016. • Action plan for development effectiveness (French only): Includes reference to private sector development and private sector engagements (though does not spell out overall approach to private sector engagement).
Netherlands	Ministry of Foreign Affairs of the Netherlands (2013), "A world to gain: A new agenda for aid, trade and investment", Ministry of Foreign Affairs of the Netherlands, The Hague, www.government.nl/files/documents-and-publications/reports/2013/04/30/a-world-to-gain/a-world-to-gain-en-1.pdf. • Refers to overarching ambitions with respect to private sector development and private sector engagement.
	Ministry of Foreign Affairs Vision on Sustainable Trade (2015, Dutch only) • Refers to private sector development and private sector engagement

Country	Policy framework and focus
New Zealand	New Zealand Ministry of Foreign Affairs and Trade (2015), "New Zealand aid programme strategic plan 2015-19", New Zealand Ministry of Foreign Affairs and Trade, Wellington, www.mfat.govt.nz/assets/_securedfiles/Aid-Prog-docs/New-Zealand-Aid-Programme-Strategic-Plan-2015-19.pdf. • Refers to private sector development and outlines ambition to engage the private sector more in development
	There is no specific private sector engagement strategy though one is under development
Norway	Norwegian Ministry of Foreign Affairs (2012), "Business creates development – What the Norwegian authorities are doing to promote private investment in developing countries, Norwegian Ministry of Foreign Affairs, Oslo, https://www.regjeringen.no/globalassets/upload/ud/vedlegg/utvikling/business_development_e899e.pdf. • Refers to private sector engagement with linkages to private sector development activities.
	Norwegian Ministry of Foreign Affairs (2014), "Working together: Private sector development in Norwegian development cooperation", Norwegian Ministry of Foreign Affairs, Oslo, https://www.regjeringen.no/contentassets/e25c842a003d4892986ce29678102593/en-gb/pdfs/stm201420150035000engpdfs.pdf. • Refers to private sector development.
Poland	No specific strategy on private sector engagement.
Portugal	Government of Portugal (2014), "Conceito estratégico da cooperação portuguesa 2014-2020 [Strategic concept of Portuguese cooperation 2014-2020]", Government of Portugal, Lisbon, http://d3f5055r2rwsy1.cloudfront.net/images/cooperacao/conctestratg1420.pdf. (Portuguese only) • Refers to private sector development and private sector engagement.
Slovak Republic	Ministerstvo zahraničných vecí a európskych záležitostí Slovenskej republiky [The Ministry of Foreign and European Affairs of the Slovak Republic] (2012), "Koncepcia zapájania podnikateľských subjektov do rozvojovej spolupráce Slovenskej republiky [Approach to the involvement of businesses in development co-operation of the Slovak Republic]", Ministerstvo zahraničných vecí a európskych záležitostí Slovenskej republiky [The Ministry of Foreign and European Affairs of the Slovak Republic], Bratislava, www.mzv.sk/documents/10182/68590/130114_koncepcia_podnikatelske_subjekty_roz_spolupraca.pdf/9835037b-9b1f-46bd-bb2e-d4748d645e95. • Refers to private sector engagement.
Slovenia	No specific strategy on private sector engagement.
Spain	Ministerio de asuntos exteriores y de cooperación [Ministry of Foreign Affairs and Cooperation] (2011), "Estrategia de crecimiento económico y promoción del tejido empresaria [Strategy for economic growth and promoting business networks]", Ministerio de asuntos exteriores y de cooperación [Ministry of Foreign Affairs and Cooperation], Madrid, www.cooperacionespanola.es/sites/default/files/crecimiento_economico_y_promocion_del_tejido_empresarial.pdf. • Refers to private sector development with links to private sector engagement.
	No specific strategy on private sector engagement.
Sweden	No specific strategy on private sector engagement.[1]
Switzerland	Swiss Agency for Development and Co-operation (2013), "Partnerships with the private sector", *Institutional Position*, Swiss Agency for Development and Co-operation, Bern. • Refers to private sector engagement.
	Swiss State Secretariat for Economic Affairs (2016), "SECO approach to partnering with the private sector", State Secretariat for Economic Affairs, Bern, www.seco-cooperation.admin.ch/themen/00960/05472/index.html?lang=en. • State Secretariat for Economic Affairs document refers to private sector engagement.
	The Swiss Agency for Development provides information regarding private sector development on its website. The website includes links to a range of policies and frameworks related to areas such as financial inclusion, making markets work for the poor and other private sector development-related activities.
United Kingdom	Department for International Development (2014), "Economic development for shared prosperity and poverty reduction: A strategic framework", Department for International Development, London, www.gov.uk/government/uploads/system/uploads/attachment_data/file/276859/Econ-development-strategic-framework_.pdf. • Refers to private sector development and private sector engagement.
United States	USAID (2014), "Partnering for impact: USAID and the private sector", United States Agency for International Development, Washington, www.usaid.gov/sites/default/files/documents/15396/usaid_partnership%20report_FINAL3.pdf. • United States Agency for International Development document refers to private sector engagement

Note: 1. Sweden has no specific strategy as it takes a decentralised approach to private sector engagement. See peer learning report for Sweden for further details: www.oecd.org/dac/peer-reviews/Peer-Learning-Country-Report-Sweden.pdf.

Private Sector Engagement for Sustainable Development:
Lessons from the DAC

ANNEX B

Definitions of terms used in the report

Additionality: "In the context of reporting on private sector instruments in DAC statistics, [the OECD-DAC Secretariat proposes that] an official transaction be considered *additional* either because of its 'financial additionality' or 'value additionality' or both. Such a transaction is *financially additional* if it is extended to an entity that cannot obtain finance from local or international private capital markets with similar terms or quantities without official support, or if it mobilises investment from the private sector that would not have been otherwise invested. It is *additional in value* if the public sector offers to recipient entities or mobilises, alongside its investment, non-financial value that the private sector is not offering and which will lead to better development outcomes e.g. by providing or catalysing knowledge and expertise, promoting social or environmental standards or fostering good corporate governance" (DCD-DAC-STAT, 2016, 7).

Bankability: A project or proposal is considered bankable if investors are willing to finance it (EPEC, n.d.).

Base of the pyramid: The base of the pyramid (BoP, sometimes referred to as the bottom of the pyramid) refers to approximately four and a half billion people who live on less than USD 8 per day at the base of the global economic pyramid. The concept of addressing the needs of people at the BoP through business was introduced in 2006 by C.K. Prahalad. Often people at the BoP are excluded from formal markets, face a lack of competition and overpay for goods and services of low quality. Under the BoP theory, poor people can benefit through the application of disruptive new technologies and inclusive business models that provide access to basic needs. Activities include engaging people at the BoP as producers, consumers and entrepreneurs to improve livelihoods and drive economic growth for communities and the private sector (BoP Global Network, 2012; BoP Innovation Center, n.d.).

Blended finance: DAC members define blended finance as "the strategic use of official funds including concessional tools to mobilise additional capital flows (public and/or private) to emerging and frontier markets" (OECD, 2016e: 3). In their work on blended finance, the World Economic Forum and OECD (2015) note that blended finance has three characteristics: leverage, the use of development or philanthropic funds to attract capital into deals (i.e. concessional finance); impact, investments that drive social, environmental and economic progress; and returns, in line with market expectations based on real and perceived risks. Given that blended finance explicitly aims to attract new participants to markets, it can be seen as a form of innovative finance.

Catalytic: The role of development organisations or aid in stimulating actions on the part of other actors such as the private sector, national governments and civil society. The term is often used to refer to catalysing additional flows for development, but a broader understanding includes catalysing other types of change, such as behavioural change and systemic change.

Corporate social responsibility: Initiatives by companies to assess and take responsibility for effects on environmental and social well-being. The term is often used to describe activities that go beyond regulatory or legal requirements. The International Organization for Standardization has set out guidelines for companies to integrate CSR into their operations (Investopedia, 2016).[10]

Debt instruments: These include transfers in cash or in kind for which recipients incur legal debt. Debt instruments include standard loans, bonds, asset-backed securities and reimbursable grants.

Development additionality: In addition to financial and value additionality, the literature on additionality often refers to development additionality. This term refers to the development impacts that arise as a result of investment that otherwise would not have occurred. In this case, one of the main rationales for partnership is that it facilitates faster, larger or better development impacts than the public or private sector would be able to achieve working alone.

Equity and shares in collective investment vehicles: Refers to investment in a country on the DAC List of ODA Recipients that is not made to acquire a lasting interest. Includes common equity, shares in collective investment vehicles and reinvested earnings.

Financial additionality: Financial additionality involves ensuring that government support is provided only when a market failure exists or a project is too risky (either in terms of location, market or innovative nature) to obtain financing from commercial investors. Financial additionality aims to not distort markets by ensuring that finance provided by government is not in competition with the private sector.

Financial risk: The possibility of financial loss as a result of an investment.

Grants: These include transfers in cash or in kind for which no legal debt is incurred by recipients. In the context of private sector engagement, DAC members provide grants directly to companies, including through challenge or innovation funds, as well as other implementing partners, such as CSOs and multilateral organisations, to carry out activities in partnership with private sector partners. Under the Creditor Reporting System, grants include standard grants, interest subsidies and capital subscriptions on deposit and encashment basis.

Guarantees and other unfunded liabilities: A guarantee refers to a risk-sharing agreement under which the guarantor agrees to pay part or the entire amount due on a loan, equity or other instrument to the lender/investor in the event of non-payment by the borrower or loss of value in case of investment. Other unfunded contingent liabilities refer to other instruments that do not constitute a flow as such but may be also collected in future.

Impact investing: According to the Global Impact Investing Network (GIIN, n.d.), impact investments are investments made into companies, organisations and funds with the intention of generating social and environmental impacts alongside financial returns. Core characteristics include: intentionality (i.e. an investor intends to have a positive impact); return expectation on capital, or at a minimum, a return of capital; a range of return expectations and asset classes; and measurement of social and environmental impacts. The ambitions of impact investing are similar to blended finance in terms of supporting positive development results while realising financial returns. However, impact investing does not explicitly seek to mobilise additional private flows, as is the case with blended finance. Impact investing can be seen as a form of innovative finance. It introduces a novel approach to an established problem, particularly in that it moves beyond traditional spending profiles for the public and private sectors. Impact investing is sometimes referred to as social investing.

Inclusive business: Efforts by the private sector to target the poor and include them into supply chains as employees, producers and business partners or through the development of affordable goods and services needed by the poor. Inclusive business has a greater focus on the profit motive than CSR activities (ADB, n.d.; Gradl and Knobloch, 2010).

Innovative finance: Innovative financing is financing that deploys proven approaches to new markets (including new customers and segments), introduces novel approaches to established problems (including new asset types) or attracts new participants to the market (such as commercially oriented investors) (Guarnaschelli et al., 2014). This broad definition includes a variety of financial tools, including mechanisms that raise funds or stimulate actions in support of international development that go beyond traditional spending approaches by either the public or private sectors (Sandor, Scott and Benn, 2009). Examples include securities and derivatives (e.g. grants, guarantees, loans, bonds and notes), results, output- or performance-based mechanisms (e.g. advanced market commitments, challenge funds and development impact bonds), voluntary contributions (donations as part of consumer purchases) and compulsory charges such as taxes (Guarnaschelli et al., 2014).[11]

Institutional or value additionality: Institutional or value additionality refers to the unique role – or comparative advantage – of a government institution in, for example, improving the development impact of an investment by influencing design or through the incorporation of standards for corporate governance and environmental and social sustainability, and providing private sector partners with access to specialised advice or networks.

Leverage: The OECD Glossary of Statistical Terms defines leverage as having exposure to the full benefits arising from holding a position in a financial asset, without having to fully fund the position with own funds.

Modalities for private sector engagement: Modalities through which private sector engagement occurs. They include knowledge and information sharing, policy dialogue, technical co-operation, capacity development and finance (Di Bella et al., 2013).

Private sector: Organisations that engage in profit-seeking activities and have a majority private ownership (i.e. not owned or operated by a government). This term includes financial institutions and intermediaries, multinational companies, micro, small and medium-sized enterprises, co-operatives, individual entrepreneurs, and farmers who operate in the formal and informal sectors. It excludes actors with a non-profit focus, such as private foundations and CSOs (Crishna Morgado et al., forthcoming; Di Bella et al., 2013).

Private sector collaboration: A subset of private sector engagement, collaboration refers to engagement with the private sector that does not include a formal contractual relationship. Collaboration occurs when potential partners explore opportunities to address development challenges. This style of engagement is characterised by low levels of formality, obligation and risk (Commonwealth of Australia, 2015a).

Private sector development: Activities carried out by governments and development organisations with the objective of promoting an enabling environment for the private sector in partner countries. Private sector development refers to the substantive nature of particular development activities (i.e. the sector targeted by development interventions). Activities include the creation of an adequate policy environment, addressing market imperfections (e.g. value chain development) and firm-level interventions (e.g. capacity building, access to finance and markets) (Crishna Morgado et al., forthcoming; Di Bella et al., 2013).

Private sector engagement: An activity that aims to engage the private sector for development results, which involve the active participation of the private sector. The definition is deliberately broad in order to capture all modalities for engaging the private sector in development co-operation from informal collaborations to more formalised partnerships. Given that the term applies to how development co-operation occurs, private sector engagement can occur in any sector or area (e.g. health, education, private sector development, renewable energy, governance, etc.). Through private sector engagement, the private sector and other participants can benefit from each other's assets, connections, creativity or expertise to achieve mutually beneficial outcomes (Crishna Morgado et al., forthcoming; Di Bella et al., 2013).

Private sector instruments: The DAC considers all financial instruments that are used to engage the private sector in development co-operation to be private sector instruments. These instruments are associated with formal private sector partnerships and create contractual obligations when used. Private sector instruments include grants, reimbursable grants, debt instruments, equity, guarantees and other unfunded liabilities (OECD, 2015b; OECD, 2014b). Private sector instruments are a subset of the finance modality for private sector engagement.

Private sector partnerships: A subset of private sector engagement, partnerships are characterised by more formal relationships (contract, memorandum of understanding, etc.) between parties and generally include higher levels of structure and obligation, including funding components (Commonwealth of Australia, 2015a).

Public-private partnerships (PPPs): A subset of private sector partnerships, according to the OECD Glossary of Statistical Terms, public-private partnerships are arrangements whereby the private sector provides infrastructure assets and services that traditionally have been provided by government, such as hospitals, schools, prisons, roads, bridges, tunnels, railways, and water and sanitation plants.

Reimbursable grants: These include contributions provided to recipients for investment purposes, with the expectation of long-term reflows at conditions specified in financing agreements. A provider assumes the risk of total or partial failure of an investment. It can also decide if and when to reclaim its investment.

Responsible business conduct: The OECD's "Policy Framework for Investment" notes that responsible business conduct entails compliance with laws, such as those on respecting human rights, environmental protection, labour relations and financial accountability, even in countries where these are poorly enforced (OECD, 2015c). CSR activities are also considered a part of responsible business conduct by the OECD. Responsible business conduct involves responding to societal expectations – in terms of environmental, social and economic outcomes – communicated by channels other than the law (e.g. by inter-governmental organisations, within the workplace, by local communities and trade unions, or via the press). The OECD has OECD Guidelines for Multinational Enterprises (OECD, 2014a)[12] on responsible business conduct and the United Nations has developed Guiding Principles on Business and Human Rights (UN, 2011).

Reputational risk: The possibility of reputational damage as a result of being associated with a particular partner or investment.

Shared value: The term refers to the result of policies and operating practices that enhance the competitiveness of a company while simultaneously advancing economic and social conditions in communities where it operates (Commonwealth of Australia, 2015a).

Notes

1. Under ISO 26000, social responsibility refers to the responsibility of an organisation for the impacts of its decisions and activities on society and the environment through transparent and ethical behaviour that contributes to sustainable development, takes into account the expectations of stakeholders, is in compliance with applicable law and consistent with international norms of behaviour, and is integrated throughout the organisation and practiced in its relationships (ISO, 2014).
2. The OECD Glossary of Statistical Terms does not define innovative finance. It does, however, define innovation co-operation as involving active participation in joint innovation projects with other organisations. These organisations may be either other enterprises or non-commercial organisations. The partners need not derive immediate commercial benefits from the venture. Pure contracting out of work, where there is no active collaboration, is not regarded as co-operation. Co-operation is distinct from open information sources and acquisition of knowledge and technology in that all parties take an active part in the work.
3. See mneguidelines.oecd.org for access to information, tools and resources relating to the promotion and implementation of the guidelines.

ORGANISATION FOR ECONOMIC CO-OPERATION AND DEVELOPMENT

The OECD is a unique forum where governments work together to address the economic, social and environmental challenges of globalisation. The OECD is also at the forefront of efforts to understand and to help governments respond to new developments and concerns, such as corporate governance, the information economy and the challenges of an ageing population. The Organisation provides a setting where governments can compare policy experiences, seek answers to common problems, identify good practice and work to co-ordinate domestic and international policies.

The OECD member countries are: Australia, Austria, Belgium, Canada, Chile, the Czech Republic, Denmark, Estonia, Finland, France, Germany, Greece, Hungary, Iceland, Ireland, Israel, Italy, Japan, Korea, Latvia, Luxembourg, Mexico, the Netherlands, New Zealand, Norway, Poland, Portugal, the Slovak Republic, Slovenia, Spain, Sweden, Switzerland, Turkey, the United Kingdom and the United States. The European Union takes part in the work of the OECD.

OECD Publishing disseminates widely the results of the Organisation's statistics gathering and research on economic, social and environmental issues, as well as the conventions, guidelines and standards agreed by its members.

OECD PUBLISHING, 2, rue André-Pascal, 75775 PARIS CEDEX 16
(43 2016 07 1 P) ISBN 978-92-64-26687-2 – 2016

www.ingramcontent.com/pod-product-compliance
Lightning Source LLC
LaVergne TN
LVHW081418110826
845149LV00010B/1783

* 9 7 8 9 2 6 4 2 6 6 8 7 2 *